OPPOSING
VIEWPOINTS®
SERIES

I Tibet

Other Books of Related Interest

Opposing Viewpoints Series
International Adoptions
US Foreign Policy
World Peace

At Issue Series
Child Labor and Sweatshops
Is China's Economic Growth a Threat to America?
Should the US Close Its Borders?

Current Controversies Series
Human Trafficking
Politics and Religion
Pakistan

"Congress shall make no law . . . abridging the freedom of speech, or of the press."

First Amendment to the US Constitution

The basic foundation of our democracy is the First Amendment guarantee of freedom of expression. The Opposing Viewpoints Series is dedicated to the concept of this basic freedom and the idea that it is more important to practice it than to enshrine it.

OPPOSING
VIEWPOINTS®
SERIES

| Tibet

Margaret Haerens and Lynn M. Zott, Book Editors

GREENHAVEN PRESS
A part of Gale, Cengage Learning

GALE
CENGAGE Learning·

Farmington Hills, Mich • San Francisco • New York • Waterville, Maine
Meriden, Conn • Mason, Ohio • Chicago

Elizabeth Des Chenes, *Director, Content Strategy*
Douglas Dentino, Manager, *New Product*

For more information, contact:
Greenhaven Press
27500 Drake Rd.
Farmington Hills, MI 48331-3535
Or you can visit our Internet site at gale.cengage.com

For product information and technology assistance, contact us at

Gale Customer Support, 1-800-877-4253
For permission to use material from this text or product, submit all requests online at
www.cengage.com/permissions

Further permissions questions can be emailed to permissionrequest@cengage.com

Articles in Greenhaven Press anthologies are often edited for length to meet page requirements. In addition, original titles of these works are changed to clearly present the main thesis and to explicitly indicate the author's opinion. Every effort is made to ensure that Greenhaven Press accurately reflects the original intent of the authors. Every effort has been made to trace the owners of copyrighted material.

Cover image Copyright © Gwoeii/Shutterstock.com.

LIBRARY OF CONGRESS CATALOGING-IN-PUBLICATION DATA

Tibet / Margaret Haerens and Lynn M. Zott, book editors.
        p. cm. -- (Opposing viewpoints)
        Summary: "Opposing Viewpoints is the leading source for libraries and classrooms in need of current-issue materials. The viewpoints are selected from a wide range of highly respected sources and publications"-- Provided by publisher. Includes bibliographical references and index.
        ISBN 978-0-7377-6666-0 (hardcover) -- ISBN 978-0-7377-6667-7 (paperback)
        1. Tibet Autonomous Region (China)--International status. 2. Tibet Autonomous Region (China)--Politics and government. 3. Human rights--China--Tibet Autonomous Region. 4. Bstan-'dzin-rgya-mtsho, Dalai Lama XIV, 1935- 5. 5. United States--Foreign relations--China. 6. China--Foreign relations--United States. I. Haerens, Margaret, editor of compilation. II. Zott, Lynn M. (Lynn Marie), 1969- editor of compilation.
        JZ1735.T53T54 2014
        320.951'5--dc23
                                                                2013047368

Printed in the United States of America
1 2 3 4 5 6 7 18 17 16 15 14

Contents

Chapter 1: How Should Tibet Be Governed?

Chapter 2: What Is the Impact of Chinese Rule in Tibet?

Chapter 3: How Should the US Engage Tibet?

Chapter 4: What Is the Best Way to Encourage Political Change in Tibet?

Why Consider Opposing Viewpoints?

> "The only way in which a human being can make some approach to knowing the whole of a subject is by hearing what can be said about it by persons of every variety of opinion and studying all modes in which it can be looked at by every character of mind. No wise man ever acquired his wisdom in any mode but this."
>
> *John Stuart Mill*

In our media-intensive culture it is not difficult to find differing opinions. Thousands of newspapers and magazines and dozens of radio and television talk shows resound with differing points of view. The difficulty lies in deciding which opinion to agree with and which "experts" seem the most credible. The more inundated we become with differing opinions and claims, the more essential it is to hone critical reading and thinking skills to evaluate these ideas. Opposing Viewpoints books address this problem directly by presenting stimulating debates that can be used to enhance and teach these skills. The varied opinions contained in each book examine many different aspects of a single issue. While examining these conveniently edited opposing views, readers can develop critical thinking skills such as the ability to compare and contrast authors' credibility, facts, argumentation styles, use of persuasive techniques, and other stylistic tools. In short, the Opposing Viewpoints Series is an ideal way to attain the higher-level thinking and reading skills so essential in a culture of diverse and contradictory opinions.

In addition to providing a tool for critical thinking, Opposing Viewpoints books challenge readers to question their own strongly held opinions and assumptions. Most people form their opinions on the basis of upbringing, peer pressure, and personal, cultural, or professional bias. By reading carefully balanced opposing views, readers must directly confront new ideas as well as the opinions of those with whom they disagree. This is not to simplistically argue that everyone who reads opposing views will—or should—change his or her opinion. Instead, the series enhances readers' understanding of their own views by encouraging confrontation with opposing ideas. Careful examination of others' views can lead to the readers' understanding of the logical inconsistencies in their own opinions, perspective on why they hold an opinion, and the consideration of the possibility that their opinion requires further evaluation.

Evaluating Other Opinions

To ensure that this type of examination occurs, Opposing Viewpoints books present all types of opinions. Prominent spokespeople on different sides of each issue as well as well-known professionals from many disciplines challenge the reader. An additional goal of the series is to provide a forum for other, less known, or even unpopular viewpoints. The opinion of an ordinary person who has had to make the decision to cut off life support from a terminally ill relative, for example, may be just as valuable and provide just as much insight as a medical ethicist's professional opinion. The editors have two additional purposes in including these less known views. One, the editors encourage readers to respect others' opinions—even when not enhanced by professional credibility. It is only by reading or listening to and objectively evaluating others' ideas that one can determine whether they are worthy of consideration. Two, the inclusion of such viewpoints encourages the important critical thinking skill of ob-

objectively evaluating an author's credentials and bias. This evaluation will illuminate an author's reasons for taking a particular stance on an issue and will aid in readers' evaluation of the author's ideas.

It is our hope that these books will give readers a deeper understanding of the issues debated and an appreciation of the complexity of even seemingly simple issues when good and honest people disagree. This awareness is particularly important in a democratic society such as ours in which people enter into public debate to determine the common good. Those with whom one disagrees should not be regarded as enemies but rather as people whose views deserve careful examination and may shed light on one's own.

Thomas Jefferson once said that "difference of opinion leads to inquiry, and inquiry to truth." Jefferson, a broadly educated man, argued that "if a nation expects to be ignorant and free . . . it expects what never was and never will be." As individuals and as a nation, it is imperative that we consider the opinions of others and examine them with skill and discernment. The Opposing Viewpoints Series is intended to help readers achieve this goal.

David L. Bender and Bruno Leone,
Founders

Glossary

ASEAN. *See* Association of Southeast Asian Nations.

Association of Southeast Asian Nations. A geopolitical and economic organization comprising the following Southeast Asian countries: Brunei, Cambodia, Indonesia, Laos, Malaysia, Myanmar (Burma), Philippines, Singapore, Thailand, and Vietnam.

Beijing The capital of the People's Republic of China (PRC). Often used in essays to stand for the government of the PRC.

Cadre A core of trained personnel around which a larger organization can be built and trained.

Central Tibetan Administration (CTA) The Tibetan government based in Dharamsala, India, established by the Fourteenth Dalai Lama after he fled from Tibet in 1959. Often referred to as the Tibetan government in exile.

CTA. *See* Central Tibetan Administration.

Dalai Clique Contemptuous term used by the Chinese government and press to refer to the supporters of the Dalai Lama and the Central Tibetan Administration.

Dalai Lama The head monk of the Gelugpa sect of Tibetan Buddhism and widely acknowledged as the spiritual and political leader of the Tibetan people. As of 2014, the Fourteenth Dalai Lama, Tenzin Gyatso, was the current Dalai Lama.

Dharamsala A city in northern India, it is the seat of the Central Tibetan Administration. Often used in essays to refer to the exiled Tibetan government.

Diaspora A group of people living outside their established or ancestral homeland.

Genocide The deliberate and systematic destruction of a racial, religious, political, or ethnic group.

Han The main ethnic group in the People's Republic of China. Many Han Chinese have settled in Tibet since the 1959 uprising and are currently the ethnic majority in Tibet.

Jasmine Revolution Depending on context, this could refer to: (1) a series of street demonstrations in Tunisia in late 2010 and early 2011 leading to the ouster of longtime president Zine El Abidine Ben Ali and the eventual establishment of democratic elections; (2) the wave of protests and demonstrations throughout the Arab world beginning with the demonstrations in Tunisia and continuing to the present; (3) the pro-democracy protests in China in February and March 2011.

Kalon Tripa The official title of the head of the Dharamshala-based Central Tibetan Administration before September 20, 2012, comparable to a prime minister.

Kashag The executive and administrative board of the Central Tibetan Administration, the Kashag's chairman is essentially the head of the Tibetan government in exile.

Kirti Monastery A Buddhist monastery in eastern Tibet that has become a center of protest by the monks and consequently subject to a political crackdown by the Chinese authorities since 2011.

Lhasa Former capital of independent Tibet and current administrative capital of the Tibet Autonomous Region (TAR) of China. Often used in essays to stand for the government of the TAR.

NGO. *See* Nongovernmental organization.

Nongovernmental organization A humanitarian or human rights group organized and administered outside of direct government control.

Panchen Lama The second most prominent Tibetan leader after the Dalai Lama in the Gelugpa sect of Tibetan Buddhism. Gedhun Choekyi Nyima was named the eleventh Panchen Lama by the Dalai Lama on May 14, 1995. He was detained by authorities of the People's Republic of China and has not been seen in public since May 17, 1995. The People's Republic of China then named Gyancain Norbu as Panchen Lama, a choice that is rejected by most Tibetan Buddhists.

PRC Abbreviation for the People's Republic of China.

Rapporteur A person designated to present official reports, particularly in the United Nations.

SAARC. *See* South Asian Association for Regional Cooperation.

Self-immolation Burning oneself alive as a form of social protest.

Sikyong The designation of the temporal head of the Tibetans after September 2012. Lobsang Sangay was elected sikyong in April 2011 for a term of five years by the Tibetan diaspora.

South Asian Association for Regional Cooperation An economic and political organization of eight countries in southern Asia: Afghanistan, Bangladesh, Bhutan, India, Maldives, Nepal, Pakistan, and Sri Lanka.

TAR. *See* Tibet Autonomous Region.

Tibet Autonomous Region (TAR) Since 1959, Tibet has been designated an "ethnic autonomous region" within the control of the People's Republic of China. Its capital city is Lhasa.

Tibetan government in exile The Tibetan government based in Dharamsala, India, established by the Fourteenth Dalai

Lama after he fled from Tibet in 1959. Officially known as the Central Tibetan Administration.

Introduction

> *"Since our utmost concern is to safeguard Tibetan Buddhist culture—rooted as it is in values of universal compassion—as well as the Tibetan language and the unique Tibetan identity, we have worked whole-heartedly towards achieving meaningful self-rule for all Tibetans."*
>
> —His Holiness the
> Fourteenth Dalai Lama of Tibet

For centuries, Tibet has had a complicated and often troubled relationship with its large and powerful neighbor, China. In recent decades, the history of that relationship has been debated by both countries—as well as by the international community—to shed light on the current political and social crises in Tibet. On one side, Tibet argues that it has always been a distinct nation with its own laws, customs, religion, language, and government. On the other side, China maintains that Tibet became part of China during the Mongol Empire and that its status as a part of China has not changed since then. For China, its version of history justifies its rule over Tibet and its treatment of Tibet protesters as terrorists and revolutionaries against the state. For Tibetans, their view of Tibetan history justifies their perception of Chinese rule as a foreign occupation and frames their protest as a fight for independence.

Tibet emerged as a sovereign country in the early years of the seventh century, becoming a strong regional power that was ruled by a series of religious emperors. During that time, Buddhism spread throughout the region and became the official religion of the state. This era lasted until 842, when the last emperor was toppled by rebellious warlords in a civil war, and the empire fragmented into smaller tribal fiefdoms.

In 1240 Mongol forces invaded Tibet, eventually incorporating the region into the Mongol Empire. Under Mongol rule, Tibet maintained some nominal power over religious and political affairs but ceded power over major administrative and political decisions to Mongol officials. The relationship between Tibet and the Mongols is central to later questions of China's legitimacy as ruler of Tibet: because China considers Mongolia to be part of China that means Mongolian rule over Tibet was actually Chinese rule. Tibetans argue that Tibet remained an independent nation that maintained fundamental authority over its administrative and political existence.

With the decline of the Mongol Empire in the mid-thirteenth century, Tibet was ruled by religious authorities and family dynasties until the rule of the Fifth Dalai Lama, Ngawang Lobsang Gyatso, who is honored for unifying central Tibet and establishing diplomatic relations with China. After his death, Tibet was administered by China as a protectorate established under the Manchurian Qing dynasty in 1721. Once again, Tibet retained a level of autonomy under Chinese rule, with the Dalai Lama assuming significant religious and political power in Tibet.

In 1912 the Qing dynasty fell and the Thirteenth Dalai Lama, Thubten Gyatso, took control of Tibet. A year later, he released a proclamation clarifying the relationship between China and Tibet. "During the time of Genghis Khan and Altan Khan of the Monghols, the Ming dynasty of the Chinese, and the Ch'ing [Qing] dynasty of the Manchus, Tibet and China cooperated on the basis of benefactor and priest relationship," he noted, adding, "We are a small, religious, and independent nation."

For the next several years, Tibet was free from Chinese influence and functioned as an independent nation. It was ruled by the Dalai Lama's government.

After the death of the Thirteenth Dalai Lama in 1933, Tenzin Gyatso, who was identified in 1937 at the age of two and
officially recognized as the next Dalai Lama in 1940, became
the Fourteenth Dalai Lama. The young man soon faced significant challenges. Communist Chinese forces invaded Tibet
in October 1950. A year later, Tibetan officials and the Chinese government ratified the Seventeen Point Agreement,
which formalized Chinese control over Tibet.

By 1956, however, minor uprisings took place in Tibet
against Chinese authority. The resistance spread, and by 1959
China began to crack down on the rebels. Fearing for his life,
the Dalai Lama fled to India in March of that year. In Dharamsala, India, just the other side of the Himalayas, he established
an office to aid the tens of thousands of Tibetan refugees who
had accompanied him or who followed later. Eventually he set
up the Tibetan government in exile, today known as the Central Tibetan Administration (CTA).

During the first few years of Chinese rule, thousands of
Buddhist monasteries were demolished by Chinese troops, and
thousands of Buddhist monks and nuns were imprisoned, tortured, and killed. Tibetan art and books were destroyed, and
the Chinese language officially replaced Tibetan in schools,
government, and popular culture. Chinese men and women
were encouraged to move to Tibet and were given preference
for jobs, promotions, and other opportunities. In many cities,
Chinese immigrants outnumber native Tibetans, leading to
concern that the Tibetan way of life is disappearing and being
supplanted with Chinese language, culture, and customs. Many
observers deem it a cultural genocide, and international groups
have rallied to help preserve and protect Tibet's rich cultural
heritage.

In March 2008 Tibetan mobs rioted in the streets of the
old capital city of Lhasa. The crackdown by Chinese forces
was immediate and harsh: monasteries and nunneries were
closed; Internet access monitored and controlled; protesters

arrested, and journalists expelled. In 2009, a wave of self-immolation protests against Chinese rule in Tibet began. More than one hundred men and women of various ages and social circumstances have set themselves on fire in Tibet, Nepal, India, and China over the past several years. Many of these protesters are Buddhist monks and nuns, and most make explicit political statements against Chinese occupation before they commit the horrifying act. Chinese officials blame the Dalai Lama for encouraging the protests, but the Dalai Lama has opposed self-immolation as a form of protest.

For both Tibet and China, Tibetan history holds the key to the country's legal status, its role in the international community, and the future relationship between the two countries. Tibetan opposition to Chinese rule is based on the belief that Tibet has historically been an independent country; therefore, China's occupation is illegitimate and a serious violation of international law. China contends that history shows that Tibet has been subject to Chinese sovereignty for centuries and remains an integral part of China.

The question of Tibet's legal status would have immediate and major political relevance. A decisive ruling on the issue would force the international community to recognize Tibet's historical and legal independence or Tibetan authorities would be faced with the ruling that Tibet is legally part of China. That is why the stakes of this historical debate are so high for many. Added to the mix is China's rank as the second largest economy in the world—power and influence that most nations cannot or do not want to oppose or antagonize.

The authors of the viewpoints in *Opposing Viewpoints: Tibet* debate the historical and legal status of Tibet under four chapter headings that ask, How Should Tibet Be Governed?, What Is the Impact of Chinese Rule in Tibet?, How Should the US Engage Tibet?, and What Is the Best Way to Encourage Political Change in Tibet? The viewpoints in this volume provide information on the US role in solving the Tibet issue, the most effective way to govern the country, and the recent wave of self-immolation protests that have shocked the international community.

OPPOSING
VIEWPOINTS®
SERIES

How Should Tibet Be Governed?

Chapter Preface

The Dalai Lama holds a unique and powerful place in Tibetan life. Tenzin Gyatso, the birth name of the current Dalai Lama, is globally recognized as the preeminent spiritual leader of the Gelugpa lineage of Tibetan Buddhism, the major religious practice in Tibet, Bhutan, Mongolia, and several other regions. He is also widely viewed as the political leader of the Tibetan people, even after being forced into exile by Chinese forces in 1959 and resigning his role as the head of Tibet's government-in-exile in 2011.

The Dalai Lama has played an integral role in raising awareness about Tibet's struggle against Chinese rule and educating people all over the world on Tibetan culture and spirituality. Yet for many Tibetans and followers of Tibetan Buddhism, the sacred role of the Dalai Lama cannot be succinctly explained.

"Since His Holiness the Dalai Lama is such an immensely revered and beloved figure, it is not easy to write about him in a casual manner, especially for a Tibetan," contends Tibetan politician Kasur Tenzin N. Tethong. "No matter what one writes, it may never satisfy those who see him as more than an ordinary being. Even on a conventional level he is not just a leader since he is both temporal and spiritual head of a people and a nation. And for devout Buddhists, he is the manifestation of the Bodhisattva of Compassion, the embodiment of the compassion of all the Buddhas, or as some might say, the essence of compassion in the universe."

Tenzin Gyatso was born on July 6, 1935, in Takster, a small village in northeastern Tibet. At the time of his birth, he was named Lhamo Thondup. It is legend that when the official search party arrived in Takster as part of the nationwide effort to identify the fourteenth manifestation of the Dalai Lama, the two-year-old boy recognized the toys of his predecessor, the thirteenth incarnation of the Dalai Lama, and claimed them as his own. The search party was also convinced by a series of prophecies and signs that Lhamo Thondup was the next incarnation, and the young boy was quickly hailed as the next Dalai Lama. He was renamed Jetsun Jamphel Ngawang Lobsang Yeshe Tenzin Gyatso—shortened to Tenzin Gyatso—but widely known as His Holiness, the Dalai Lama.

The new Dalai Lama encountered resistance from Chinese authorities from the beginning of his reign. A powerful Chinese warlord in the region, a Muslim known as Ma Bufang, put the young boy and his family under house arrest to prevent him from traveling to Lhasa, the capital of Tibet. Only after the Tibetan government purchased safe passage for the young man was he allowed to travel to Lhasa and be formally installed as the Dalai Lama in 1940. He spent the next several years in intense studies, preparing for his role as a political and religious leader.

After China invaded Tibet in 1950, the Dalai Lama was thrust to the forefront of an unfolding political and humanitarian crisis. While Chinese forces began to take control of Tibetan institutions and clash with Tibetan monks—battles that often resulted in violence and bloodshed—the Dalai Lama attempted to work with the Chinese to preserve Tibet's religious heritage and rich culture as well as to protect the human rights of Tibetan people. However, by the late 1950s it was clear that Chinese rule meant oppression in the eyes of most Tibetans. The Dalai Lama's leadership was increasingly viewed as a threat to the Chinese government.

A failed Tibetan uprising in 1959 led to the Dalai Lama's escaping to India in March 1959. In Dharamshala, in northern India, he established the Tibetan government-in-exile to aid the thousands of Tibetan refugees also fleeing Chinese rule.

Over the next decades, the Dalai Lama launched a worldwide campaign to raise awareness of the crisis in Tibet. He appealed to the United Nations on behalf of Tibet, pleading for international attention to human rights abuses there and for assistance for Tibetan refugees. He supported the establishment of hundreds of Tibetan monasteries and nunneries; founded the Tibetan Institute of Performing Arts to preserve Tibetan culture; facilitated the study of Tibetan history, culture, and religion by opening the Library of Tibetan Works and Archives; opened the Central Institute of Higher Tibetan Studies; and oversaw the transition to a democratic government through the creation of a democratically elected parliament. In 2011 the Dalai Lama stepped down as the formal head of state but continues to travel all over the world on behalf of the Tibetan people.

The political role of the Dalai Lama is one of the subjects of the following chapter, which debates how Tibet should be governed. Other viewpoints evaluate the impact of Chinese rule, the prospects of Tibetan independence or political autonomy, and the legitimacy of the Central Tibetan Administration (CTA).

> *"[Tibet should] surrender to Beijing to-day rather than tomorrow because the current conditions are better than they will be in future. And in doing so, try to . . . [make] a case for an alignment of interests between the Dalai Lama and Beijing."*

Tibet Should Be Governed by China

Francesco Sisci

Francesco Sisci is a newspaper columnist in Italy. In the following viewpoint, he contends that the cause of Tibetan independence has not evolved over the past few years; in fact, Chinese rule is more entrenched than ever, and the cultural and spiritual bonds between the Tibetans and Han Chinese residing in Tibet are stronger. Sisci argues that the death of the aging Dalai Lama will exacerbate these trends and widen the divide between Tibetans living abroad and those remaining within the country's borders. It may be the best option for Tibet to surrender to Chinese rule in order to gain any advantage it can from Beijing, Sisci maintains, but in reality, Tibetan leadership will most likely ignore this option as a futile path that will only cause it to lose any leverage in negotiations.

As you read, consider the following questions:

1. How many suicides across the historical region of Tibet have there been in the past few years, according to Sisci?

2. What marginalized group does Sisci compare Tibetans with?

3. What is as a major obstacle in surrendering to Chinese rule, in the author's opinion?

Is there a future for the Tibetan cause? After two years of protests and more than 100 suicides across the historical region of Tibet, it is hard to see any real evolution in the cause of Tibetan independence or even autonomy.

Certainly, Chinese rule in Tibet has been tarnished by the wave of self-immolations that shows no signs of receding. Beijing has imposed new rules on satellite dishes, banning reception of subversive broadcasts from India and other countries. It has slapped new restrictions on the use of inflammables and applied new controls on monasteries and checks on the activities of monks.

These measures are bound to push more common Tibetans, even those who might be more sympathetic to the government, toward the cause of those committing suicide. But China being what it is—and unlikely to radically change in the next few years—even if the suicides were to number 1,000 or 10,000 among Tibetans in China, who represent less than 0.5% of the population, that would hardly shake Beijing's resolve in its rule of the region.

This, for Beijing, is an issue of cold-blooded political calculation, and time is on its side. Despite the potential growing sympathies for the self-immolators, there are some very important trends at work in the region.

Key Trends in Tibet

Tibetans in Tibet are becoming increasingly different from those living outside of Tibet. They listen to different music, watch different TV programs, and even speak a language that

The Han Chinese in Tibet

Tibet is a region of central Asia that the People's Republic of China (mainland China) declares is part of China. To many Tibetans, however, it is an independent country occupied by China. The United Nations (UN) has declined to accuse China of occupying an independent country but, along with human-rights organizations, has formally expressed concern over many Chinese practices in the region, particularly its crackdowns on dissent.

One major human rights concern is China's systematic settlement of Tibet by large numbers of imported Chinese immigrants of Han (Chinese majority) ethnicity. This has been interpreted as an effort to absorb the distinctive Tibetan culture and people; some Tibetans fear that the Chinese culture will override their own. Nongovernmental organizations (NGOs) testified to the United Nations Human Rights Council on March 30, 2007, that systematic Han settlement of Tibet is a form of ongoing "cultural genocide." The Chinese government denies systematic Han settlement of Tibet.

Global Issues in Context, "Tibet:
Conflicts with China," 2013. www.gale.cengage.com.

is becoming distinct on the two sides of the Himalayan highlands. Moreover, even without taking into account the position of the government, normal Han Chinese (the vast majority of the population) are warming to their Tibetan "possessions".

Tibetan living Buddhas are roaming China, spreading their religious message and being wined and dined by rich and powerful Chinese in search of some form of spirituality to feel connected to. To them, traditional Chinese Buddhism is losing steam and appeal, while new Western Christianity is too foreign and at odds with their traditional mindset. Tibetan Buddhism is both authentic and reverberates with old beliefs. To these people, who might even be sympathetic to the Tibetan plight, the loss of Tibet would be like losing a piece of the country's soul. This bond of common Chinese to Tibet is becoming deeper, and it goes well beyond nationalistic attachments to a stretch of land or a rock out in the water [i.e., Taiwan].

In this sense, a new identity seems to be developing for both Tibetans, who are becoming more integrated into China and increasingly detached from their brethren living in India or abroad, and for Han Chinese, who feel closer to Tibetan culture and religion and who find in the Himalayas a new source of spiritual life after decades of communist or capitalist materialism.

The self-immolation taints and humiliates those in charge of Beijing's rule in Tibet, but does not change the basic facts: the greater integration of Tibetans into Beijing's China and the warm feelings many Chinese have for Tibet. Conversely, in a way, the suicides help to strengthen these deeper trends. Tibetans will be more cut off from foreign influence and face more Chinese authorities, and thus naturally will have a stronger sense of belonging to China's Tibet, which they may dislike but they can't avoid.

In a way, it is like the situation with Native Americans: they may have disliked and fiercely opposed colonization, but in the end, more than ever they belong to the United States. Meanwhile, the Han Chinese—even when they are sympathetic to the Tibetan cause—will develop stronger feelings for Tibet, and thus deep in their souls will be more reluctant to let it go.

The Dalai Lama Factor

In this situation, the death of the Dalai Lama will make things worse for the cause of Tibet. Beijing will choose its own Dalai Lama, and the Tibetans outside of Tibet will choose theirs.

The sentiment in Tibet will be split. No doubt many—if not most—people will support the Dalai Lama who resides outside of Tibet, but it is also likely that a minority, which might grow, will listen to the Beijing-appointed Dalai Lama, especially if he manages to more closely address the worries and concerns of the Tibetans in Tibet, while the Dalai Lama outside of Tibet becomes more and more detached from the qualms and sentiments of Tibetans in Tibet.

This trend is not likely to be reversed even in the case of massive democratization in China. Conversely, a more democratic China could feel stronger about Tibet, and thus resent direct or indirect attempts to break it apart from the rest of the country. Then a democratic China, answering more directly to the will of the people, would have less room to maneuver in dealing with Tibetans in exile.

Unless one believes there could be a major breakup of China with a civil war and all its trappings, the prospect of an improved climate for exiled Tibetans to talk to Beijing is worsening by the day—also, paradoxically, because of the self-immolations.

The Options

What then would I say if I were an adviser to the Dalai Lama? I would tell him that, generally speaking, there are two options on the table:

1. Work toward a civil war in China that could blow up the country, and thus create an opportunity to carve out Tibet's independence or greater autonomy. The possibility of success for this is slim and depends on the general thrust of the countries in the region: are they willing to foment a civil war in China that could kindle chaos in the whole world? In reality, this is still an option, although chances are becoming thinner, as the potential global costs of a civil war in China grow by the day.

2. Surrender to Beijing today rather than tomorrow because the current conditions are better than they will be
   in future. And in doing so, try to extract as much as
   possible by presenting a case for an alignment of interests between the Dalai Lama and Beijing. This would
   mean forfeiting decades of fighting and dreams of independence or great autonomy, but it would avoid the
   greater split between Tibetans within and outside of Tibet. It will be difficult because the people out of Tibet
   have lived all their lives according to these dreams, and
   to smash them in return for nothing will be very painful
   and hard to explain—especially since the possibility, albeit small, of massive civil war in China still exists.

Realistically, chances are that, as has happened so far, the
Tibetan leadership will not clearly choose between the two
grand options, and this will continue to stifle their initiatives.
They could opt, as they have done, for small tactical cam-
paigns, such as the Dalai Lama's tours, supporting protests in
Tibet, confronting Chinese authorities where they can, and
spreading to far-flung parts of the world followers of the
Dalai Lama who can undermine China's image and soft power.

Facing Reality

All these small initiatives have not dented Beijing's rule in Tibet and have actually, as we saw, reinforced the deeper integration of Tibetans into China. They make real sense only in
case of an all-out effort to bring down unitary China, something that is not likely to happen any time soon, as we saw.
Meanwhile, Tibetans out of Tibet will lose the leverage to negotiate.

This, to me, reinforces the need for the second course of
action. But will His Holiness the Dalai Lama accept this analysis and prevail over his many counselors? He is the only one
who is able to do it, but can he really?

| "*The Tibetan people are entitled to exercise their right of self-determination.*"

Tibet Should Be Fully Independent and Self-Governing

Tibet Justice Center

The Tibet Justice Center (TJC) is a legal and educational organization that works toward the realization of an independent Tibet. In the following viewpoint, the TJC outlines the history of Tibet to show that it has always been an independent, sovereign nation. Chinese claims that Tibet is part of China are illegitimate and based on a treaty signed through coercion; therefore, such an agreement is not legally binding. It is clear that the invasion of Tibet by Chinese forces constitutes an illegal occupation. Therefore, the Tibetan people are entitled to exercise their right of self-determination, as set out in international law. As evidenced by historical records, Tibet should be fully independent and free from Chinese rule.

As you read, consider the following questions:

1. When did the People's Republic of China (PRC) invade Tibet, according to the Tibet Justice Center?

"Briefing Paper: Centenary of the 1913 Independence Proclamation by His Holiness the XIIIth Dalai Lama," Tibet Justice Center, 2013. Copyright © 2013 by Tibet Justice Center. All rights reserved. Reproduced by permission.

2. In what year of the last century did Tibet formally expel Chinese troops, as stated by the author?

3. In what country does the exiled Tibetan government reside, according to the Tibet Justice Center?

Tibet was an independent, sovereign nation when the armies of the People's Republic of China ("PRC") entered Tibet in 1950. Tibet at that time practiced all the attributes that define statehood under international law. Even the PRC does not dispute that the Tibetans are a distinct people who in 1950 occupied a distinct territory.

Tibet also had a fully functioning government, headed by the Dalai Lama. That government, free from outside interference, administered the welfare of the Tibetan people through a civil service, judicial and taxation systems, as well as through a postal and telegraph service, and a separate currency.

The Tibetan government controlled the borders and issued passports to its people, documents that were recognized internationally.

Sovereign Tibet entered into treaties with other states, including Great Britain, Ladakh [a region of India], Nepal and Mongolia. Tibet also entered into a treaty with China in 822, and negotiated as an equal sovereign with China and Great Britain at the Simla Conference of 1913–14.

The Seventeen Point Agreement of 1951, which the PRC claims resolved Tibet's status, is not a legally binding agreement. The Agreement was signed when armies of the PRC occupied large parts of Tibet, the Tibetan representatives did not have authority to sign the Agreement on behalf of Tibet, and it was signed under threat of further military action in Tibet. A treaty concluded under such circumstances is legally void under international law and thus of no effect.

Under international law, once a state exists, it is legally presumed to continue as an independent state unless proved otherwise. The historical evidence not only fails to prove otherwise, but affirmatively demonstrates that Tibet has always been an independent state, despite periods during which it was influenced to varying degrees by foreign powers.

Historical Independence of Tibet

Tibet indisputably was an independent state before the 13th century. Tibet was the most powerful sovereign nation in Asia in the 8th century and entered into a treaty with China in 822. For the next 300 years, there was no official contact between Tibet and China.

In the 13th century, Tibet came under Mongol dominance several decades before the Mongols conquered China militarily and established the Yuan Dynasty. Tibet was not part of China before the Mongol conquest and during the Yuan Dynasty was administered separately by the Mongols through local Tibetan rulers. Nor did Tibet lose its sovereignty during this period. The relationship between Tibet and the Mongols was a unique priest-patron relationship known as *cho-yon*. The relationship involves a reciprocal legitimation of complementary forms of authority.

During Tibet's "Second Kingdom," from 1349 to 1642, Tibet was a secular kingdom free of both Mongol and Chinese control. Emperors of the Chinese Ming Dynasty nominally granted titles to certain Tibetan officials but exercised neither de jure [legal] nor de facto [actual] control over Tibetan affairs, nor over the successive changes in the Tibetan government. Successive Ming Emperors exercised no control over the Dalai Lamas, who later took control of Tibet.

Tibet at the Time of the Qing Dynasty

During the Qing Dynasty, the Dalai Lamas and the Manchu Emperors reestablished the *cho-yon* relationship. The Emperors' representatives in Lhasa, the *Ambans*, initially served only as liaisons to the Emperor. In 1793, the Emperor purported to grant the Ambans power to exercise control over

The UN Charter and the Right of Self-Determination

A half-century ago, much of the world was made up of colonies and dependent Territories ruled by a small number of colonial Powers. In 1945, the Charter of the United Nations proclaimed "the respect for the principle of equal rights and self-determination of peoples" as one of its basic purposes. Self-determination means that the people of a colony or a dependent Territory decide about the future status of their homeland. In the following decades, more than 80 colonial Territories became independent as a result of self-determination. Other Territories chose free association, or integration with an independent State. The process by which these Territories exercised their right to self-determination is known as decolonization.

United Nations,
"Questions and Answers," 2013. www.un.org.

Tibet's external affairs, but this was presented to the Eighth Dalai Lama as a suggestion, not an exercise of Imperial power. Within a few decades, the Ambans exerted virtually no influence in Tibet and the Qing Emperors stopped providing the protection that was their side of the *cho-yon* relationship, effectively ending it.

Tibet formally expelled the last garrisoned troops of the Qing Emperor in 1911, an unmistakable act of sovereignty, and repatriated them to China in 1912. China's Kuomintang Government invited Tibet to join the Nationalist Republic, but Tibet declined. The Nationalist Government attempted unilaterally to assert control over Tibet until 1918 and then again beginning in 1931, but failed. In 1949, Tibet expelled the last remaining Chinese representatives.

The Occupation

Tibet was an independent country at the time of the Chinese invasion in 1950 with a government headed by the political and religious institution of the Dalai Lama. The State of Tibet continues, despite China's illegal occupation, through the work of the legislative, judicial, and executive branches of the Tibetan Government, now in exile in India. The Dalai Lama served as Head of State with executive functions organized under the cabinet, or Kashag, until 2011, when political authority devolved to the Sikyong, or Political Leader of the Kashag. Under the current constitution, legislative authority rests in an elected parliament, and an independent judiciary has been established.

Tibet Is Entitled to Self-Determination

Even if Tibet had not been an independent nation in 1950, the Tibetan people are nonetheless entitled to exercise their right of self-determination. International law recognizes the right of peoples to self-determination; that is, *"the right freely to determine, without external interference, their political status and to pursue their economic, social and cultural development."* The Tibetans are unquestionably a "people" to whom the right of self-determination adheres. They are entitled to choose independence from the PRC, autonomy within the PRC, or any other political status.

The Tibetan people are entitled to exercise their right of self-determination as against the PRC's claim of territorial integrity because the PRC has not acted as the legitimate government of the Tibetan people. A government's legitimacy derives from a people's exercise of the right of self-determination and from its conduct in accordance with its obligation to protect and promote the fundamental human rights of all of its peoples, without discrimination. The PRC's government in Tibet was imposed on the Tibetans by force, not by an exercise of self-determination. Moreover, the PRC has persistently and systematically abused the human rights of Tibetans through repression of religion, population transfer, birth control policies, discrimination, destruction of the environment, involuntary disappearances, arbitrary arrest, arbitrary torture, and arbitrary executions.

The People's Republic of China is therefore not the legitimate government of the Tibetan people and has no claim of territorial integrity to assert against the Tibetans' right of self-determination.

International Values

A consideration of the fundamental values of the international community also weighs heavily in favor of enforcing the Tibetans' right to self-determination. A non-militarized independent Tibet would enhance peace and security in Asia by serving as a buffer zone between the two most populous nations in the world—India and China—who have gone to war only after the PRC stationed troops in Tibet along the Indian border. The Tibetans' exercise of self-determination will also promote the international values of respect for human rights and fundamental freedoms. The PRC has openly and officially abused Tibetan human rights in an apparent effort to marginalize the Tibetans as a people. Only the exercise of self-determination by the Tibetans will restore respect for the Tibetans' human rights and fundamental freedoms.

> *"I call on Beijing to accept our Middle Way Policy, which seeks genuine autonomy for Tibetans within the framework of the Chinese constitution."*

Tibet Should Be Governed by a "Middle Way" Approach

Lobsang Sangay

Lobsang Sangay is a legal scholar, political activist, and the political leader of the Tibetan people, known as the Sikyong (formerly the Kalön Tripa). In the following viewpoint, he applauds the smooth transition of political power in the Tibetan government-in-exile from the Dalai Lama to a democratically elected leader. Sangay calls on the Chinese government in Beijing to accept the Middle Way Policy, a proposal that seeks political autonomy for Tibetans within the framework of the Chinese constitution. This is imperative, he argues, in order to protect the unique Tibetan culture and fundamental human rights. The Central Tibetan Administration (CTA) is ready to send envoys to resume a dialogue with Chinese authorities despite Chinese attempts to denigrate the Dalai Lama and China's further oppression of the Tibetan people.

Lobsang Sangay, "Statement on the 53rd Anniversary of Tibetan Uprising Day," Central Tibet Administration, March 11, 2012. Copyright © 2012 by Central Tibet Administration. Reproduced by permission.

As you read, consider the following questions:

1. How many Tibetans does the Central Tibetan Administration represent, according to Sangay?

2. What percentage of Tibetan high school and college graduates are unemployed, as reported by the author?

3. According to Sangay, on what day did the Dalai Lama issue a historic statement regarding his reincarnation?

Today, on the 53rd anniversary of the Tibetan National Uprising Day and the fourth anniversary of the 2008 mass protests in Tibet, I offer tribute to the brave people who have sacrificed so much for Tibet. Despite fifty-three years of occupation by the People's Republic of China (PRC), the Tibetan spirit and identity inside Tibet remains unbroken.

On this occasion, I pay homage to His Holiness the Dalai Lama for his vision, leadership and benevolence. I also pay my deepest respect and gratitude to our elders for their contribution and tireless effort that have sustained our movement's growth and dynamism over the past fifty years.

A Smooth Transition

One year ago [in 2011], when His Holiness the Dalai Lama announced the transfer of his political power to a democratically elected leader, Tibetans were apprehensive and implored him to reconsider. Today, the world recognizes and applauds His Holiness' vision and magnanimous decision. Tibetans are making a smooth transition with the free, fair and multi-candidate 2011 parliamentary and Kalon Tripa [the political leader of the Tibetan government-in-exile] elections that involved exile and diaspora Tibetans in over forty countries.

I am deeply honored by the spiritual blessings, legitimacy, political authority and continuity bestowed upon me by His Holiness the Dalai Lama. In his statement at my inauguration ceremony on August 8th, 2011, His Holiness said "when I was young, an elderly regent Takdrag Rinpoche handed over Sikyong (political leadership) to me, and today I am handing over Sikyong to young Lobsang Sangay. . . . In doing this, I have fulfilled my long-cherished goal."

I am also enormously moved by the solidarity and endorsements from Tibetans inside Tibet during the elections and since assuming my political post. I have had many deeply moving encounters with hundreds of Tibetans from Tibet as they generously offered their blessings and support.

Blessed by the historic transfer of political power from His Holiness, empowered by the mandate received from the people, and buoyed by the support and solidarity from Tibetans inside Tibet, I can say with pride and conviction that the Central Tibetan Administration [CTA] legitimately represents and speaks for all six million Tibetans.

Chinese Control of Tibet

Beijing's view that a generational change in leadership may weaken the Tibetan freedom movement has not and will never materialize. The resiliency of the Tibetan spirit combined with a coming generation of educated Tibetans will provide dynamic leadership and sustain the movement till freedom is restored in Tibet.

If the Chinese government's claim that Tibetans enjoy freedom and equality are true, then it should allow democratic, transparent, free and fair elections in Tibet. In the fifty-three years of Chinese occupation, no Tibetan has ever held the Party Secretary post of the so-called Tibet Autonomous Region (TAR). Chinese hold the majority of the decision-making positions in all branches of the government and constitute more than fifty percent of the public sector workforce. Seventy percent of the private sector enterprises are owned or operated by Chinese. Forty percent of Tibetan high school and college graduates are unemployed.

The Tibet issue concerns far more than the rights and welfare of six million Tibetans. It impacts the entire planet. The unique Tibetan culture, with its rich language, spirituality and history must be protected. The Tibetan plateau is the 'world's third pole' as it contains the largest ice fields outside the two poles. Tibetan glaciers, the source of ten major rivers, affect the lives of more than 1.5 billion people. Billions of dollars worth of mineral resources are exploited annually to fuel China's economy. Decades of logging have reduced Tibet's pristine forest cover by half. Clearly, the management of this global common, and the Tibetan people's traditional role as its stewards, ought to be a planetary concern.

When China invaded Tibet in 1949, it promised to usher in a 'socialist paradise.' In actuality Tibetans are treated as second-class citizens. When Tibetans gather peacefully and demand basic rights as outlined in the Chinese constitution, they are arrested, fired upon and killed as in the January 23–24th [2012] peaceful protests when Chinese were celebrating their new year. The Communist Party cadre members in the TAR have been ordered to prepare for a "war" against the Tibetan protestors.

In stark contrast, in Wukan (Guangdong Province), protests by Chinese people lasted weeks, their grievances were addressed, one of the protest leaders was appointed in a leadership position for the village, and provincial authorities even supported free village elections.

A Cultural Genocide

Intellectuals, artists and leaders in Tibet are being arbitrarily arrested and imprisoned. Thousands of pilgrims recently returning from India have been detained and many have disappeared. Tibetans, including monks and nuns, are forced to denounce the Dalai Lama and attend patriotic re-education classes. Foreigners and international media are barred from Tibetan areas.

The Meaning of the Middle Way Approach

The Tibetan people do not accept the present status of Tibet under the People's Republic of China. At the same time, they do not seek independence for Tibet, which is a historical fact. Treading a middle path in between these two lies the policy and means to achieve a genuine autonomy for all Tibetans living in the three traditional provinces of Tibet within the framework of the People's Republic of China.

His Holiness, the 14th Dalai Lama of Tibet,
"His Holiness's Middle Way Approach for
Resolving the Issue of Tibet," 2013. www.dalailama.com.

A Chinese scholar recently observed there are "more Chinese than Tibetans, more police than monks, more surveillance cameras than windows" in Lhasa, the capital city of Tibet. The entire region is under undeclared martial law.

China has built many airfields in Tibet, stationed many more divisions of the PLA [People's Liberation Army], begun expanding the railway line to the borders of neighboring countries, and dispatched thousands of paramilitary forces into Tibetan areas. Tibet has become one of the most militarized areas in the region.

Today, there is no space for any conventional protests such as hunger strikes, demonstrations and even peaceful gatherings in Tibet. Tibetans are therefore taking extreme actions such as the one by 26 Tibetans who have committed self-immolations since 2009. His Holiness the Dalai Lama and the CTA have always discouraged such drastic actions. However, despite our pleas, Tibetans continue to self-immolate with 13 cases already in 2012. Fault lies squarely with the hardline leaders in Beijing; so does the solution. The self-immolations are an emphatic rejection of the empty promises of the so-called 'socialist paradise.'

The Middle Way Policy

The Tibetan struggle is not against the Chinese people or China as a nation. It is against the PRC government's policies. China must acknowledge the depth of the problems in Tibet and understand they cannot be solved through violence.

To address the tragedy in Tibet, I call on Beijing to accept our Middle Way Policy, which seeks genuine autonomy for Tibetans within the framework of the Chinese constitution and as proposed in the Memorandum and Note of 2008 and 2010 respectively. Hong Kong and Macao have been granted a high degree of autonomy. Despite resistance from Taiwan, China has offered Taiwan more autonomy. Why are Tibetans still not granted genuine autonomy as stipulated in the Chinese constitution?

We hope that China's upcoming leaders will initiate genuine change, and that they find the wisdom to admit the government's long-standing hardline policy in Tibet has failed. We have chosen to move down a mutually beneficial path even though Tibet historically enjoyed independent status and Tibetans have the right to self-determination according to international law. Concerned Chinese citizens and intellectuals should make an effort to seek the truth and understand why Tibetans are protesting and self-immolating. Dialogue and a peaceful resolution to the Tibet issue are in the best interest of China, the Chinese people and Tibetans.

We stand ready to send envoys to resume the dialogue process even though the Chinese envoy belonging to the United Front Work Department has of late invested far more energy traveling around the world and making outrageous attacks on His Holiness the Dalai Lama and the CTA led by the Kalon Tripa. In the process they have actually further internationalized the Tibet issue.

A Plea to the United Nations

A key reason for creating the United Nations was the pursuit of human rights. I urge the UN to live up to its objective and address the crisis in Tibet by appointing a Special Rapporteur and visiting Tibet.

The international community and media must send a fact-finding delegation into Tibet to remove the veil of censorship and disinformation campaign. "Even Pyongyang (North Korea) has an international media presence, which is not the case in Lhasa," says Reporters Without Borders.

I appeal to the officials and member states of ASEAN [Association of Southeast Asian Nations] and SAARC [South Asian Association for Regional Cooperation] to include the Tibet issue in your agenda given Tibet's geopolitical and environmental significance affecting billions of Asians. A China that is able to address the Tibet issue will make it a more peaceful neighbor and contribute to harmony and stability in the region.

Time for Action

To my fellow Tibetans, now is the time to show solidarity and support with our brothers and sisters in Tibet. We must give education top priority so that educated and community-minded Tibetans will provide dynamic leadership and sustain the Tibetan movement till freedom is restored in Tibet. The Kashag [the governing council of the Tibetan government-in-exile] would like to request that mantras and prayers be recited every Wednesday for those who have sacrificed their lives for the Tibetan cause. Younger Tibetans should embrace and celebrate our proud heritage and identity by wearing, speaking and eating Tibetan every Wednesday.

Let us make 2012 a Tibet Lobby Year. In this Tibetan New Year, I call upon all Tibetans and friends to reach out to elected representatives at the state and national levels in your countries. Invite and educate them about Tibet and the efforts of His Holiness the Dalai Lama and the CTA. Generate debate about Tibet and get legislations passed in support of Tibet and the Tibetan people. Initiate activities that raise the profile of Tibetan democracy and visibility of Tibetan political leadership and the CTA.

The fourteenth Kashag will make maximum efforts to realize our larger goal, as well as take steps to prepare the Tibetan people and institutions for the 21st century under the guiding principles of unity, innovation and self-reliance. The Kashag again urges all Tibetans and friends participating in various solidarity activities to ensure that the activities are undertaken peacefully, in accordance with local laws, and with dignity. Please remember non-violence and democracy are two of our constant principles.

Appreciation for Support

The Tibetan people and current Kashag are extremely blessed to have the continuing presence and wisdom of His Holiness, the great 14th Dalai Lama. The Kashag extends absolute support to the historic statement issued on September 24, 2011 by His Holiness concerning his reincarnation. We believe His Holiness alone has the right to determine his reincarnation, and that the communist government of China has absolutely no say or role in this matter.

I would like to take this occasion to thank all governments, especially the governments of United States, Europe and Asia, organizations, Tibet Support Groups, and individuals who have supported the Tibetan people. Your support is greatly appreciated. I also call on our old and new friends alike to reinvigorate the Tibet Support Groups around the world. We need you more than ever at this critical time. The

Kashag would also like to acknowledge the full cooperation of the Chitue Lhentsok and looks forward to a productive partnership in serving Tibet and Tibetan people.

I am also happy to express the Tibetan people's deepest and continued gratitude to the government and people of India for their generous hospitality and kindness over the past five decades. My appreciation has grown tremendously since becoming the political head of the Tibetan people. Hardik Shukriya!

Lastly, to our dear brothers and sisters in Tibet, we would like to say that you are in our hearts and prayers every day. We will walk side by side with you till freedom is restored for Tibetans and His Holiness the Dalai Lama returns to Tibet. I pray for the long life of His Holiness the Dalai Lama. May our long cherished goal of freedom and reuniting in the Land of Snows be realized soon!

"[The Dalai Lama] has been a remarkably effective leader in an extremely difficult cause for more than 50 years."

The Dalai Lama Is an Effective Leader of Tibet

Isabel Hilton

Isabel Hilton is a broadcaster and journalist and the author of The Search for the Panchen Lama. *In the following viewpoint, she offers an appreciation of the Dalai Lama as he announces his political retirement in 2011. Hilton argues that he has been a very effective political leader for the Tibetan people in difficult times, inspiring his fellow Tibetans to remain strong and resilient in the face of unrelenting pressure from Chinese forces. The Dalai Lama has also succeeded in bringing international attention to Tibet's plight and has provided a moral authority in the face of oppression and the systematic destruction of Tibetan culture and spiritual tradition, she contends. The transition to a democratic leadership for the Tibetan people is necessary to avoid the real threat of interference by Chinese authorities, Hilton maintains.*

As you read, consider the following questions:

1. Which incarnation of the Dalai Lama is the current Dalai Lama, as reported by Hilton?

2. When did the institution of the Dalai Lama begin in Tibet, according to the author?

3. According to Hilton, when was it announced that the new Penchen Lama had been found in Tibet?

The Dalai Lama's announcement of his political retirement, made in his exile capital of Dharamsala in Northern India yesterday [March 9, 2011], was news that many of his followers knew was coming but that most did not want to hear.

An Inspiring and Effective Leader

The 14th incarnation has been a remarkably effective leader in an extremely difficult cause for more than 50 years. He has given the plight of the Tibetan people both an international profile and a moral authority that all of Beijing's efforts to discredit him have failed to dent. Without him, the Tibetans might have become just another fragmented and forgotten group of exiles clinging to a dying culture. With him, they have proved resilient and tenacious, and have benefited from the global recognition that he has earned.

It has been a remarkable story. But, as he himself has often pointed out, although his followers believe their dalai lamas to be *bodhisattvas* (effectively, emanations of the Buddha), in their human incarnations, they are undoubtedly mortal. The 14th Dalai Lama is 75 and, like any good leader, he worries about succession.

The Dalai Lama is not the only one to think about what happens when he leaves the stage. China's rulers have blamed him for all their difficulties in colonising and pacifying Tibet. Most recently, they laid the uprising in 2008 at his door, despite ample evidence that Chinese policy was at the root of the discontent.

Ironically, the more the Chinese attacked him, the more popular he became, both inside and outside Tibet. In exile, he has achieved an almost unquestioned leadership that is far more widely accepted than it had been historically in Tibet, with its religious and political quarrels. If the Dalai Lama now stands for Tibet and all Tibetans, the Chinese largely have themselves to blame.

History of the Dalai Lama Tradition

The institution of the dalai lama began in 17th-century Tibet, when the 5th dalai lama became king. Like his successors, he belonged to the celibate Gelugpa sect, and the succession was determined by reincarnation. A new dalai lama was identified by religious authorities, who used dreams, divination and interrogation to settle on their choice. A new incarnation was typically found at the age of two or three, and there followed a long period of regency until the dalai lama took on his political role. Many never made it—dying, suspiciously, on the eve of assuming power.

From the current Dalai Lama's perspective, there is no obvious solution to the succession that meets the demands of his dual religious and political role. Even in old Tibet, the system had its drawbacks: long regencies were inherently unstable and despite the dominance of the religious establishment, the choice of dalai lama depended on a potent combination of high politics and profound faith and was often disputed. In the current circumstances, those drawbacks are so dangerous in the unequal contest between Beijing and Dharamsala that the Dalai Lama has often suggested that the institution has outlived its usefulness and that it should end with him.

The Panchen Lama Affair

His doubts are well founded. When the 10th Panchen Lama, the second most senior figure in the Dalai Lama's school of Buddhism, died in Tibet in 1989, the Chinese Communist Party saw in the search for his reincarnation an opportunity to exercise their control of Tibet's religious establishment. When the Dalai Lama announced in 1995 that a boy had been

The Panchen Lama

The Panchen Lama is an important holy figure in the Gelugpa sect of Tibetan Buddhism, which has dominated religious life in Tibet since the eleventh century. A remote, isolated mountain country that sits between India and China, Tibet has had a long history of adversity with China, which has claimed it as its own. A deeply spiritual land where most citizens are subsistence farmers, Tibet had no army when China invaded it in 1950. For a time, Tibetans were allowed to practice their religion freely, but harsh new policies incited a 1959 rebellion. The movement was brutally suppressed by the Chinese military, and Tenzin Gyatso, the Dalai Lama who played a key role in the uprising, was forced to flee to India.

The tenth Panchen Lama died in 1989, and [Gyaincain] Norbu was born on February 13, 1990, in Lhari country. Tibetan Buddhism dictates that a young boy born soon after the Panchen Lama's death shall succeed him, and the Dalai Lama recognized Gedhun Choekyi Nyima, born in April of 1990, as the eleventh Panchen Lama on May 14, 1995. The Chinese authorities deemed that choice invalid, and selected Norbu in a sacred vase ceremony at the Zhaxi Lhunbo Lamasery in Xigaze in the Tibet Autonomous Region. His name was drawn from a golden urn, and then approved by the state council. Both boys have rarely been seen since then. Nyima is thought to be under virtual house arrest with his parents, and has been termed the world's youngest political prisoner by human rights watchdog groups. It is thought that the majority of Tibetan Buddhists consider him the rightful Panchen Lama, even though it is Norbu's portrait that is displayed in every temple in Tibet.

Gale Biography in Context,
"Gyaincain Norbu," 2004. www.gale.cengage.com.

found in Tibet, Beijing was furious. The boy and his family disappeared and Beijing insisted on a rigged procedure to choose a substitute who is now widely shunned in Tibet as the "Chinese Panchen". He could, however, be wheeled out by Beijing as the ultimate authority on the choice of the next Dalai Lama.

The affair stands as a warning of Chinese intentions when the Dalai Lama dies. He has tried to keep the Chinese at bay by insisting that, if he were to reincarnate, he would do so in exile. They have responded, in effect, that his reincarnation is none of his business. A Chinese government spokesman recently insisted, eccentrically, that not only must the Dalai Lama be reborn, he must be reborn in China.

Tibetans have grown used to the bizarre sight of an officially atheist party-state issuing ever more precise rules for reincarnation; a sense of irony has never been the Party's greatest virtue. But the political sub-text is real enough: Tibet's profound religious traditions have proved an immovable obstacle to the acceptance of Beijing's rule. Having failed to destroy the religion in Tibet, Beijing now believes that controlling Tibet's Buddhist leaders is the key to pacifying the people. Rather than see a successor play that role, the Dalai Lama would prefer the entire institution to bow out.

If he were ever to return to Tibet, he once told me, he would regard his job as done and would wish to retire to the life of a simple Buddhist monk. Painfully, he regards his own political leadership as a failure in one important respect: that his policy of non-violence and compromise with Beijing has yielded no result.

The Failure of China's Strategy

Sporadic talks in the past decade between the Dalai Lama's representatives and the Beijing government have led nowhere and the tenor of Beijing's rhetoric against the exiled leader has grown steadily more vituperative. Even the announcement of his retirement yesterday was described in Beijing as a trick. The Chinese government continues to characterise him as a "separatist", despite the fact that he has long accepted that Chinese rule over Tibet is irreversible and that what he wants is meaningful autonomy.

It is difficult to avoid the conclusion that Beijing never wanted to negotiate in good faith, but by failing to talk seriously, China has lost the opportunity to reach a mutually beneficial settlement that only the Dalai Lama could deliver. Without him, they calculate, Tibet's international profile will disappear and the one figure who can unite Tibetans in Tibet and Tibetans in exile will be gone. From Beijing's perspective, their troubles would be over. It is, at best, a gamble: without the Dalai Lama's restraining influence, the hostility towards Chinese rule that erupted in 2008 could well grow rather than diminish.

A Democratic Future

Having failed in his ambition to reach a settlement while he was still in a position to do so, the Dalai Lama now believes that it is time to consolidate institutions that can legitimately represent Tibetans in exile and perhaps serve as a moral stimulus for a distant future democracy in Tibet. Yesterday's announcement is the culmination of a project to consolidate a democratic system that would enable him to step back from a political role he long wanted to leave.

It has proved a difficult challenge: Tibetans have accepted with great reluctance the idea that anyone could be a better leader than the Dalai Lama, or that any elected leader would merit the respect that he does. It has taken some determination on his part to force his followers to share his modernising impulse and embrace secular politics.

Until now, the elected prime minister of the exile government has been a monk, but in the final round of the forthcoming election this year, all of the candidates are laymen, a radical shift in the self image and political maturity of today's Tibetans in exile. It remains to be seen how much of the Dalai Lama's role the winning candidate can assume: the elected leader of the Tibetan exile community is unlikely to enjoy the same access to the White House as the Dalai Lama.

However it plays out, yesterday's announcement marks a moment of profound transition. No future dalai lama is likely to play this dual religious and political role again, and no future dalai lama is likely to be asked to carry the fate of an entire people in crisis on his shoulders. The 14th Dalai Lama will be a hard act to follow.

> *"The Dalai Lama is the leader of the Free Tibet movement [but] when it comes to advancing that goal, he has been a resounding failure."*

The Dalai Lama Is Not an Effective Leader of Tibet

Andy Lamey

Andy Lamey is an educator, journalist, and author. In the following viewpoint, he contends that although the Dalai Lama is an internationally beloved figure, he has largely been a failure when it comes to his position as leader of the Free Tibet movement. The Dalai Lama's passive and nonviolent approach to Chinese oppression in Tibet has been counterproductive and has failed to move negotiations with China forward. Western supporters have been complicit in this approach, encouraging Tibetan exiles to perpetuate a failed strategy. The Dalai Lama has acknowledged that he has not succeeded in securing Tibetan autonomy from China. His best course of action is to abandon his political role and to let a new generation take up the fight.

As you read, consider the following questions:

1. What year did Canada grant the Dalai Lama citizenship, according to Lamey?

Andy Lamey, "Stop the Lama Love-In," *MacLean's*, November 25, 2009. Copyright © 2009 by Andy Lamey. All rights reserved. Reproduced by permission.

2. What novel first depicted the mystical Tibetan paradise of Shangri-La, as reported by the author?

3. To what South African political figure does Lamey compare the Dalai Lama?

Everyone loves the Dalai Lama. Just how much was on display two weeks ago [in mid-November 2009] when the Tibetan religious leader paid a visit to the town of Tawang in northeastern India. Ethnic Tibetans travelled to the frontier outpost from all over the sub-continent in order to venerate the 74-year-old monk at a huge outdoor rally. "He is our god, he is the living Buddha. A glimpse of the Dalai Lama is like getting spiritual power inside you," said one participant in explaining the extraordinary adulation the Dalai Lama inspires. Here in Canada, our view is not so different. When the Dalai Lama travelled to Vancouver, Calgary and Montreal last month, tens of thousands crowded into stadiums to hear his message of universal compassion. The rapturous reception was in keeping with our decision in 2006 to grant him citizenship, the highest honour Canada bestows on foreign leaders. The Dalai Lama's other admirers include the U.S. government, which awarded him the Congressional Gold Medal, and the Nobel Peace Prize committee. The general feeling of Lama-mania was summed up by TV star Sandra Oh, who co-hosted one of his Canadian appearances. "He's a rock star! Rock star! Seriously, a rock star!"

A Failed Leader

Yet if the Dalai Lama is a rock star, does he live up to the hype? His spiritual teachings contain elements of illogic and intolerance that would not be accepted from any other religious figure. That these go unnoticed is largely due to the way Tibetan Buddhism functions as a spiritual Rorschach blot onto which Westerners project their hopes and desires. The primary problem, however, is political. In addition to being a spiritual figure, the Dalai Lama is the leader of the Free Tibet movement. And when it comes to advancing that goal, he has been a resounding failure. Uncritical adulation legitimizes the Dalai Lama's failed leadership and undermines one of the great political causes of our time.

It's not hard to understand the Dalai Lama's appeal. At first glance he holds out the promise of religious belief purged of any trace of fundamentalism. When it comes to modern science, for example, he has said that when it conflicts with Buddhist teachings, Buddhism should be revised. Other theological statements he has made, such as his declaration that "any deed done with good motivation is a religious act," bespeak a similarly open-minded temperament.

Contradictory Philosophy

But this progressive outlook can sometimes turn out to be illusory. Consider the teaching for which he may be best known, his doctrine of universal compassion. As he has written, "nonviolence applies not just to human beings, but to all sentient beings—any living thing that has a mind." That belief is why, when the Dalai Lama was invited to a fundraising luncheon for a monastery in Wisconsin in 2007, the organizers expected him to ask for a vegetarian meal. Instead they watched him happily ingest pheasant and veal. "He pretty much lapped up every single plate that he had put in front of him," one tablemate later said. "He loves food; he likes good food." The Dalai Lama, it turns out, is vegetarian at his official residence in India but not while travelling. But a doctrine of compassion that switches on and off depending on geography is not much of a doctrine at all.

The Dalai Lama's position on same-sex relationships is equally puzzling. "I look at the issue at two levels," he told the *Vancouver Sun* in 2004. Homosexuality is perfectly acceptable for non-believers. And for people who look to the Dalai Lama for guidance? "For a Buddhist, the same-sex union is engaging in sexual misconduct." The double-sided approach is rooted in a traditional method of explaining discrepancies between schools of Buddhism, whereby the Buddha is said to have taught different things to different people. But as with the doctrine of compassion, the Dalai Lama's considered view ends up being a sloppy relativist mess. Or at least it does in the West, where he is obliged to state his view regarding non-Buddhists. When addressing Buddhists directly the Dalai Lama's position is less complicated—and more crudely prejudicial.

The Goldilocks Solution

This side of the Dalai Lama's spiritual teachings is never subject to criticism. Why? One possibility is that the Dalai Lama solves a specifically Western problem. In the 19th century the shared religious values that once permeated our civilization began a "long withdrawing roar," as Matthew Arnold [nineteenth-century British poet and culture critic] put it. Any religion one adopts now is merely one possibility among many, a reality that drains each of its explanatory value and force. An infatuation with the Dalai Lama is the Goldilocks solution for a culture that finds traditional religion too hot and atheism too cold. His exoticism marks him as authentic, and subjecting his teachings to critical scrutiny is beside the point, as there is never any chance we are going to engage his teachings seriously enough to be challenged by them. We instead want to bask in his distant spiritual glow.

The Dalai Lama's appeal is arguably closely entwined with the peculiar fascination the West has long exhibited for all things Tibetan. When Europeans discovered Tibet, it was a remote kingdom that had never been colonized and still seemed to exist in the ancient past. It quickly became a land of fantasy. Shangri-La, the mystical Tibetan paradise, was first depicted in the 1933 novel *Lost Horizon* by James Hilton. In the late 1930s the Nazis sent an expedition to Tibet, hoping to find an ancient race of Aryans. After the devastation of the Second World War, European intellectuals imagined Tibet as "an unarmed society." As Buddhist scholar Donald Lopez notes, these myths have a common source. In each case, "the West perceives some lack within itself and fantasizes that the answer, through a process of projection, is to be found somewhere in the East."

Tibet and Western Celebrity

This process continued after China invaded Tibet in [1950], and many Tibetans were driven into exile. When the Beatles recorded *Tomorrow Never Knows,* John Lennon wanted his voice to sound like "the Dalai Lama on the mountain top." Remember the cuddly and eco-friendly Ewoks in *Return of the Jedi*? The language they spoke was modified Tibetan. Today Tibet is embraced by celebrities ranging from the Beastie Boys to action hero Steven Seagal. "The Dalai Lama gave me a spiritual blessing that would not have been given to anyone who was not special," Seagal announced in 1996. "I don't think he has given such a blessing to another white person."

Just how special Seagal is became clear in 1997 when Tibetan religious authority Penor Rinpoche declared him to be the reincarnation of a 17th-century lama. However ridiculous it may seem to imagine the star of *Exit Wounds* and *Pistol Whipped* as a holy being, Seagal's anointment symbolizes the transformation Tibetan Buddhism has undergone as it has come in contact with new patrons and admirers in the West. Rather than something "out there," Tibetan culture is influenced by how Westerners engage with it.

Political Failures

Unfortunately, on a political level, that influence has been highly negative. Seeing how requires understanding the different and at times conflicting roles the Dalai Lama now plays in addition to being the spiritual head of Tibetan Buddhism. No-

The Dalai Lama

Jetsun Jamphel Ngawang Lobsang Yeshe Tenzin Gyatso, the fourteenth Dalai Lama and leader of the Tibetan Buddhist community, is considered to be one of the most revered and influential spiritual leaders in the world. His lifelong efforts to campaign peacefully on behalf of Tibetan human rights while in exile have inspired human rights and peace activists worldwide. His efforts toward world peace, environmental harmony, and the liberation of oppressed peoples everywhere have made him a symbol of tolerance and respect, as well as a champion of nonviolent resolution to political conflicts. He has also been largely responsible for a growing interest in Tibetan culture and religion in the United States.

"The Fourteenth Dalai Lama,"
Religious Leaders of America.
Farmington Hills, MI: Gale, 2013.

where is this more true than in regard to his position as leader of the Tibetan government in exile, and the Free Tibet movement more broadly.

Since China invaded Tibet it has engaged in a campaign of ruthless repression. It is official government policy to "end the nomadic way of life" of traditional Tibetans and to forcibly resettle them. Tibetans who protest are subject to show trials and torture. Opposing China's actions has rightly been characterized as a moral struggle on the scale of the movement against apartheid or for Indian independence. Unfortunately, the Dalai Lama is the equal of neither [South African civil rights activist] Nelson Mandela nor [leader of the Indian independence movement Mohandas] Gandhi. He is as miscast as the head of Tibet liberation as the pope would have been leading the struggle against [Nazi leader Adolf] Hitler. Under his leadership political goals have inevitably taken a back seat to spiritual ones.

Tibet Compared to South Africa

A comparison to South Africa is instructive. One of the most inspiring moments in the struggle against apartheid came during the famous Rivonia trial when Nelson Mandela, faced with a possible death sentence, spoke from the prisoner's dock. Freedom, he said, was "an ideal which I hope to live for and to achieve. But if needs be, it is an ideal for which I am prepared to die." Mandela's speech galvanized the anti-apartheid movement. The Dalai Lama's pronouncements, by contrast, could not be less defiant. "I practise certain mental exercises which promote love toward all sentient beings, including especially my so-called enemies." Mandela endorsed an international boycott of South African athletes. When China hosted the 2008 Olympics, the Dalai Lama sent Beijing his regards. "I send my prayers and good wishes for the success of the event." If the Dalai Lama had led the struggle in South Africa, apartheid would still be in effect. Unsurprisingly, [60] years after the occupation, Tibet is still not free.

At times it seems that is what Western Tibetophiles would unknowingly prefer. In the words of actor Richard Gere, a long-time advocate of Tibetan independence, "Many of us constantly remind our Tibetan friends, 'You must maintain that sense of uniqueness and that genuine cultural commitment to non-violence. If you pick up arms and become like the Palestinians, you'll lose your special status.'"

The Dalai Lama's Passive Approach

Leave aside the fact that the moral case for armed resistance in Tibet is as strong as it was in France under German occupation. There are many steps an independence movement can take that fall short of violence, measures such as strikes or boycotts. The Dalai Lama has thrown himself into none of these, which are all at odds with loving one's enemy. This approach is reinforced by his Western admirers, who are drawn to the myth of Tibet as an unarmed society (even though Tibet has fought armies from Mongolia, Nepal and Britain). The overall effect of his staunchest Western fans therefore has been to reward and perpetuate an approach to Tibetan independence that has no hope of ever succeeding.

To be fair, his Holiness has begun to admit as much. "I have to accept failure; things are not improving in Tibet," he said last November [2008], acknowledging the "death sentence" Tibetans continue to face under Chinese rule. His supporters stress the awareness he brings to the Tibetan cause and the anger Chinese officials express whenever the Dalai Lama receives an audience with a Western leader. But after a certain point, awareness has to give way to action.

The New Generation

Slowly, another political faction is taking form. As one young Tibetan who has spent his entire life in exile in India said in March [2009], "We do not get anything from China. So some young people want to go to a little bit of violence—not to kill anyone but to do something so that China knows they will actively [resist]." Such a view is in keeping with the position of the Tibetan Youth Congress, which stands for "the total independence of Tibet even at the cost of one's life." If progress is to ever be made on Tibet, these approaches need to be taken seriously. But that can only happen if the Dalai Lama steps aside as a political leader, and lets a new generation take over [He did step aside in 2011].

First, however, public perception of the Dalai Lama needs to change. As it stands, when people turn their attention to him, they do so in the spirit of answering [Beatle] John Lennon's call to "turn off your mind, relax, and float downstream." The outcome of this lazy attitude is to reinforce the

Dalai Lama's leadership and his counterproductive efforts to free his people. The basic problem was summed up by the Dalai Lama himself when he stated, "I find no contradiction at all between politics and religion." So long as the Dalai Lama is regarded as a figure of both spiritual and political liberation, his efforts to make the first goal happen will ensure the second never does.

> *"The people of Tibet will continue to regard the Central Tibetan Administration as their true authority."*

The Central Tibetan Administration Should Be Tibet's Legitimate Ruling Body

Kelsang Gyaltsen

Kelsang Gyaltsen is a special envoy of the Dalai Lama. In the following viewpoint, he attempts to clarify some of the misconceptions and controversy surrounding the Dalai Lama's decision to transition to a democratically elected political leadership in the form of the Central Tibetan Administration (CTA). The Dalai Lama's plan should be understood "as a demonstration of his faith in the political maturity and determination of the Tibetan people" and that the CTA is ready to fully represent and serve the Tibetan people in the political realm. The fact that the Dalai Lama and the Tibetan people have vested the CTA with this power means that they are Tibet's legitimate ruling body. Once the CTA has reached a satisfactory agreement with China, the CTA will be dissolved and the Tibetans inside of Tibet will take over administration duties, the author maintains.

Kelsang Gyaltsen, "The Legitimacy and Role of the Central Tibetan Administration," The Office of Tibet, June 20, 2011. Copyright © 2011 by The Office of Tibet. All rights reserved. Reproduced by permission.

As you read, consider the following questions:

1. What was the Central Tibetan Administration (CTA) initially titled, according to Gyaltsen?

2. How many Tibetan refugees followed the Dalai Lama into exile in India, as reported by the author?

3. What two countries does Gyaltsen identify as part of China's "core interests"?

O nce again the small Tibetan world in exile seems to be torn apart by an emotional and political dispute over the devolution of the administrative and political powers of His Holiness the Dalai Lama to the democratically elected organs of the Tibetan Administration and over the change of the title of "Tibetan Government-in-Exile" in Tibetan language to "Central Tibetan Administration". The tone of the debate is often agonizing, bitter and self-lacerative reflecting the self-pitying and self-dramatizing psyche of some of the debating Tibetans. This way, the discourse has so far been rather self-defeating and demoralizing than helping to clarify and better understand the issues involved.

The Administration's Aim

The primary objective of these changes is to ensure the continuity of the Tibetan freedom struggle led by the Central Tibetan Administration. The changes demonstrate the political will and determination of the Tibetan leadership to continue the Tibetan freedom struggle as long as it takes by laying the ground and positioning itself in a way that allows it to function and operate in future in spite of any vicissitude in the international political environment. The devolution of His Holiness the Dalai Lama's political powers to the democratically elected leaders of the Central Tibetan Administration is to be seen and understood as a demonstration of his faith in the political maturity and determination of the Tibetan people— especially the younger generation of Tibetans inside Tibet as well as in exile.

This is, I believe, the central message that the changes embody and the Tibetan leadership wishes to convey to Tibetans, the Chinese leadership and the international community.

This is clearly an initiative that demonstrates strength, self-confidence, determination and resourcefulness on the part of the Tibetan leadership. This spirit of steely political will and commitment to our freedom struggle is evident from the amendments to the Charter of the Tibetans in exile. The amendments make it clear that His Holiness will fully vest the Central Tibetan Administration and in particular its democratic leadership organs with the powers and responsibilities formerly held jointly by him and the Central Tibetan Administration to represent and serve the whole people of Tibet. The new preamble to the Charter underlines "safeguarding the continuity of the Central Tibetan Administration as the legitimate governing body and representative of the whole Tibetan people, in whom sovereignty resides". It also enshrines Tibet's position as a sovereign nation from the early 2nd century BC until the invasion by the People's Republic of China in 1951, and His Holiness the Dalai Lama's efforts in introducing democratic reforms after coming into exile in India since 1959.

The Ruling Body of the Tibetan People

Against this background there is absolutely no basis to contend that the Central Tibetan Administration has given up the mandate to represent the entire people of Tibet as a consequence of the recent changes. On the contrary, politically and legally the legitimacy of the Central Tibetan Administration to represent the Tibetan people has been strengthened by completing the process of democratization. Sovereignty resides with the people of Tibet. Consequently, the more complete

the Tibetan authority is constituted by a free and fair democratic process the greater its legitimacy to represent the aspirations of the Tibetan people.

On arriving in exile in India in 1959 His Holiness the
Dalai Lama stated that wherever he and his Kashag (Cabinet)
are the people of Tibet will continue to consider them as their
government and true representatives. His Holiness established
the Central Tibetan Administration under the direction of his
Kashag in order to actively pursue the cause of Tibet, to draw
the attention of the world to the tragedy unfolding in Tibet
and to seek the international community's help in protecting
the Tibetan people as well as to look after about 80,000 Tibetan refugees arriving in India.

The official name of this administration has been "The
Central Tibetan Administration of His Holiness the Dalai
Lama". Our official letter-head and seal display this descrip-
tion. In all our external relations we introduce ourselves as the
Central Administration of His Holiness the Dalai Lama. We
did not seek legal or political recognition as "the Tibetan
Government-in-exile" as such confident that the Tibetan
people regarded His Holiness and the Central Tibetan Administration as their government and true representatives, this being the continued source of legitimacy.

The Will of the Tibetan People

Right from the beginning of our exile it seems that it has been
of great importance to His Holiness to make clear that he is
not staking any claims to power and rule for himself and/or
his administration. The primary task of our exile has always
been to seek justice for Tibet and to restore the basic rights
and freedoms of the Tibetan people.

There is no serious dispute about the fact that the people
of Tibet will continue to regard the Central Tibetan Administration as their true authority as long as the leadership of the
Central Tibetan Administration has the blessing and full back-

A Political Transition

An aide to the Dalai Lama announced in November 2010 that the leader would renounce his position as the head of the Tibetan government in exile at the next meeting of the exiled government's parliament. He would retain his role as the spiritual leader of Tibet. A spokesman explained that it was the leader's hope to make the Tibetan movement less centered on the Dalai Lama and thus less vulnerable to Chinese pressure. On 10 March 2011, the Dalai Lama announced that he would indeed relinquish his role as head of the government, ceding his position to the winner of the elections held on 14 March, when the Tibetan parliament next met.

The results of the election, in which Tibetans around the world were allowed to vote, were announced on 27 April 2011 in Dharamsala, India. The winner, with 55 percent of the vote, was Lobsang Sangay (1968–), a legal scholar and Research Fellow at the East Asian Legal Studies Program at Harvard Law School. He plans to move to Dharamsala and continue to pursue the goals established by the Dalai Lama.

*Global Issues in Context, "Tibet:
Conflicts with China," 2013. www.gale.cengage.com.*

ing of His Holiness the Dalai Lama—irrespective of the recent changes. Only the people of Tibet can decide whom they consider and accept as their true representatives. Although Tibetans inside Tibet cannot vote in the democratic elections of the Central Tibetan Administration, they demonstrate their support and adherence to it in in many ways, despite the severe risks of doing so. If an individual Tibetan, living in freedom in exile, decides to consider the Central Tibetan Administration from now on as a non-governmental organisation because of the recent changes—this is his or her personal free choice and decision alone.

Every Tibetan with some sense of political awareness and responsibility knows that one of His Holiness' political credos has always been: To hope for the best and to prepare for the worst. In the past decades of our freedom struggle the Tibetan people and the cause of Tibet have been served well by and have benefited immensely from this wise approach of His Holiness.

China's Response

It is no news to people with an interest in China that Beijing has been demonstrating in recent time that it won't be shy about playing hardball to safeguard what it claims to be its "core national interest". China watchers attest to a reawakened resolve on the part of the Chinese leadership to do whatever it takes to defend "core interests" such as their claims regarding Taiwan and Tibet. The Central Party School strategist, Gong Li, is quoted as saying "Beijing should not yield a single inch as far as Taiwan and Tibet are concerned". It is an open secret that China uses coercive diplomacy on other countries to assert its position. A good example is, among a growing number of other cases and signs, of the use and impact of China's coercive diplomacy are Nepal's recent policies towards our compatriots in that country. It is common knowledge that the acceptance and adherence to the principle of "One China Policy" is a precondition by China for the resumption of diplomatic relations with any government in the world.

Looking ahead and taking precautionary measures with the aim to coping with any political vicissitudes in the future is an act of responsible and prudent political leadership.

New Challenges

Far from appeasing China these initiatives by His Holiness represent a number of new challenges to the Chinese leadership. First of all they dismember the basic tenets of the Chinese justification propaganda narrative of "liberation", as well as of their claim that the Dalai Lama is bent on the "restoration of feudal theocracy" and they bring into question their calculations on the issue of reincarnation. On a more practical and concrete political level His Holiness the Dalai Lama is once again making unambiguously clear that he has no personal demands to make to the Chinese leadership. He is putting the rights and welfare of the Tibetan people right in the forefront of the Sino-Tibetan dialogue. He is making clear that the fundamental issue that needs to be resolved is the faithful implementation of genuine autonomy that will enable the Tibetan people to govern themselves in accordance with their own genius and needs.

By devolving his political powers His Holiness is once again emphasising that his engagement for the cause of Tibet is not for the purpose of claiming certain personal rights or political positions, nor in order to stake claims for the Tibetan administration in exile. Once a satisfactory agreement with China is reached, the Central Tibetan Administration will be dissolved and it is the Tibetans in Tibet who should carry the main responsibility of administering Tibet.

Even after the amendments of the Charter the political mandate of the Central Tibetan Administration continues to be to serve the people of Tibet by acting as the free voice of our captive nation and representing the people's aspirations in the wider world. In contrast to the Chinese Communist Party, it makes clear beyond any doubt that the Central Tibetan Administration is not seeking power to rule over Tibet. The sole task and purpose of the Central Tibetan Administration is no more and no less than to lead the struggle for the rights of the Tibetan people to freely determine their own affairs and to live in freedom and dignity in the land of snow that is our home.

The change of the title in Tibetan of our Administration only reemphasises this basic position of the Central Tibetan Administration without renouncing the legitimacy of representing the voice and aspiration of the people of Tibet.

"We have made great efforts to strengthen our democratic institutions to serve the long-term interests of the six million Tibetans . . . because democracy is the most representative system of governance."

Tibet Should Adopt a Democratic Government

Tenzin Gyatso, the Dalai Lama

Tenzin Gyatso is the fourteenth Dalai Lama, the spiritual leader of the Tibetan people. In the following viewpoint, he underscores the urgent need to reform Tibet's political system and announces his retirement as Tibet's political leader. Strengthening Tibet's democratic institutions is essential to meet the needs of Tibetans and to ensure that there is stability and viability for the country's survival, he contends. No system of government can be healthy and responsive if it does not have the participation of the people. He maintains that it is better for him to bow out now while he is still productive and can provide guidance to the new democratic government if needed.

As you read, consider the following questions:

1. Who was the first of forty-two Tibetan kings, according to Gyatso?

2. Which incarnation of the Dalai Lama was the first to have both spiritual and political leadership of the Tibetan people, as reported by the author?

3. On what date did the Dalai Lama explain his decision to step down from political leadership?

It is common knowledge that ancient Tibet, consisting of three provinces (Cholkha-sum) was ruled by a line of forty-two Tibetan kings beginning with Nyatri Tsenpo (127 BCE), and ending with Tri Ralpachen (838 CE). Their rule spanned almost one thousand years. During that time, Tibet was known throughout Inner Asia as a powerful nation, comparable in military power and political influence with Mongolia and China. With the development of Tibetan literature, the richness and breadth of the religion and culture of Tibet meant that its civilisation was considered second only to that of India.

The Decline of Tibet

Following the fragmentation of central authority in the 9th century, Tibet was governed by several rulers whose authority was limited to their respective fiefdoms. Tibetan unity weakened with the passage of time. In the early 13th century, both China and Tibet came under the control of [Mongol leader] Genghis Khan. Although Drogon Choegyal Phagpa restored the sovereignty of Tibet in the 1260s, and his rule extended across the three provinces, the frequent change of rulers under the Phagmo Drupas, Rinpungpas and Tsangpas over the next 380 years or so resulted in a failure to maintain a unified Tibet. The absence of any central authority and frequent internal conflicts caused Tibet's political power to decline.

Since the Fifth Dalai Lama's founding of the Ganden Phodrang Government of Tibet in 1642, successive Dalai Lamas have been both the spiritual and temporal leaders of Tibet. During the reign of the Fifth Dalai Lama, all the 13 myriarchies or administrative districts of Tibet enjoyed political stability, Buddhism flourished in Tibet and the Tibetan people enjoyed peace and freedom.

During the late 19th and early 20th centuries, Tibet not only lacked adequate political governance, but also missed the opportunity to develop effective international relations. The Thirteenth Dalai Lama assumed temporal power in 1895, but was compelled to flee to Mongolia and China in 1904, due to the invasion of British forces, and to India in 1910, when the Manchu Chinese invaded. Once circumstances allowed him to return to Tibet, the Thirteenth Dalai Lama re-asserted Tibetan sovereignty in 1913. As a result of what he had learned in exile, the Thirteenth Dalai Lama introduced modern education and made reforms to strengthen the government of Tibet. Although these steps produced positive results, he was unable to fulfil his overall vision, as is evident from his last political testament of 1932, the year before his death. Despite the lacklustre political leadership and short-comings of the regents and their administrations, the Ganden Phodrang Government has on the whole provided stable governance for the last four centuries.

Reforming Tibet's Political Institutions

Since I was young, I have been aware of an urgent need to modernize the Tibetan political system. At the age of sixteen, I was compelled to assume political leadership. At that time I lacked a thorough understanding of Tibet's own political system, let alone international affairs.

However, I had a strong wish to introduce appropriate reforms in accordance with the changing times and was able to effect some fundamental changes. Unfortunately, I was unable to carry these reforms any further due to circumstances beyond my control.

Soon after our arrival in India in April 1959, we set up departments with Kalons (Ministers) in charge of education, preservation of culture and the rehabilitation and welfare of the community. Similarly, in 1960, aware of the importance of democratization, the first Commission of Tibetan People's Deputies was elected and in 1963 we promulgated the Draft Constitution for a Future Tibet.

No system of governance can ensure stability and progress if it depends solely on one person without the support and participation of the people in the political process. One man rule is both anachronistic and undesirable. We have made great efforts to strengthen our democratic institutions to serve the long-term interests of the six million Tibetans, not out of a wish to copy others, but because democracy is the most representative system of governance. In 1990, a committee was formed to draft the Charter for Tibetans-in-Exile and a year later the total strength of the Assembly of Tibetan People's Deputies (ATPD), the Tibetans in exile's highest law-making body, was increased. In 1991, the Eleventh ATPD formally adopted the Charter for Tibetans-in-Exile and assumed all legislative authority. Given the limitations of our life in exile these are achievements of which we can be proud.

In 2001, the Tibetan people elected the Kalon Tripa, the political leader, directly for the first time. Since then, I have been in semi-retirement, no longer involving myself in the day-to-day administration, but able to dedicate more time to general human welfare.

Embracing Democratic Reforms

The essence of a democratic system is, in short, the assumption of political responsibility by elected leaders for the popular good. In order for our process of democratization to be

© Cartoonstock.com.

complete, the time has come for me to devolve my formal authority to such an elected leadership. The general lack of experience and political maturity in our democratic institutions has prevented us from doing this earlier.

Given that the line of Dalai Lamas has provided political leadership for nearly four centuries, it might be difficult for Tibetans generally and especially those in Tibet to envisage and accept a political system that is not led by the Dalai Lama. Therefore, over the past 50 years I have tried in various ways to raise people's political awareness and encourage their participation in our democratic process.

In my 10th March statement of 1969, for instance, I stated, "When the day comes for Tibet to be governed by its own people, it will be for the people to decide as to what form of government they will have. The system of governance by the line of the Dalai Lamas may or may not be there. In particular, the opinion of the forward-looking younger generation will be an influential factor."

Similarly, in my 10th March statement of 1988, I stated, "As I have said many times, even the continuation of the institution of the Dalai Lama is for the people to decide." Since the 1980s, I have repeatedly advised the Kashag, [the governing council], ATPD and the public that Tibetans should take full responsibility for the administration and welfare of the people as if the Dalai Lama were not there.

A Change in Leadership

I informed the Chairman of the Thirteenth ATPD and the then Chief Justice Commissioner that I should be relieved of functions related to my political and administrative status, including such ceremonial responsibilities as the signing of bills adopted by the legislative body. However, my proposal was not even considered. On 31st August 2010, during the First Tibetan General Meeting (organized by ATPD), I explained this again in detail. Now, a decision on this important matter should be delayed no longer. All the necessary amendments to the Charter and other related regulations should be made during this session so that I am completely relieved of formal authority.

I want to acknowledge here that many of my fellow Tibetans, inside and outside Tibet, have earnestly requested me to continue to give political leadership at this critical time. My intention to devolve political authority derives neither from a wish to shirk responsibility nor because I am disheartened.

On the contrary, I wish to devolve authority solely for the benefit of the Tibetan people in the long run. It is extremely important that we ensure the continuity of our exile Tibetan administration and our struggle until the issue of Tibet has been successfully resolved.

"A Sound System of Governance"

If we have to remain in exile for several more decades, a time will inevitably come when I will no longer be able to provide leadership. Therefore, it is necessary that we establish a sound system of governance while I remain able and healthy, in order that the exile Tibetan administration can become self-reliant rather than being dependent on the Dalai Lama. If we are able to implement such a system from this time onwards, I will still be able to help resolve problems if called upon to do so. But, if the implementation of such a system is delayed and a day comes when my leadership is suddenly unavailable, the consequent uncertainty might present an overwhelming challenge. Therefore, it is the duty of all Tibetans to make every effort to prevent such an eventuality.

As one among the six million Tibetans, bearing in mind that the Dalai Lamas have a special historic and karmic relationship with the Tibetan people, and as long as Tibetans place their trust and faith in me, I will continue to serve the cause of Tibet.

Although Article 31 of the Charter spells out provisions for a Council of Regency, it was formulated merely as an interim measure based on past traditions. It does not include provisions for instituting a system of political leadership without the Dalai Lama. Therefore, amendments to the Charter on this occasion must conform to the framework of a democratic system in which the political leadership is elected by the people for a specific term. Thus, all the necessary steps must be taken, including the appointment of separate committees, to amend the relevant Articles of the Charter and other regulations, in order that a decision can be reached and implemented during this very session.

As a result, some of my political promulgations such as the Draft Constitution for a Future Tibet (1963) and Guidelines for Future Tibet's Polity (1992) will become ineffective. The title of the present institution of the Ganden Phodrang headed by the Dalai Lama should also be changed accordingly.

Periodical and Internet Sources Bibliography

The following articles have been selected to supplement the diverse views presented in this chapter.

Tenzin Dorjee	"Why Lhakar Matters: The Elements of Tibetan Freedom," Phayul.com, January 15, 2013.
Dagny Dukach	"Beijing Begins to Debate the Tibet Issue," Council on Foreign Relations, August 1, 2013. www.cfr.org.
The Economist	"Bold New Proposals," June 22, 2013.
Richard Finney	"Tibetan 'Independence Day' Marked," Radio Free Asia, February 12, 2013. www.rfa.org.
Tenpa Dhargyal Gashi	"The Final Step in a Democracy," Phayul.com, January 28, 2013.
Vijay Kranti	"How Tibetans Are Losing Their Focus and Unity," Tibet Sun, February 6, 2013. www.tibetsun.com.
Peter Lee	"Tibet's Only Hope Lies Within," *Asia Times*, May 7, 2011.
Lian Xiangmin	"Tibet's Path to Democracy," *China Daily*, May 26, 2011.
Maura Moynihan	"The Myth That Can Devastate Tibet," *Deccan Chronicle* (South India), May 18, 2013.
Lobsang Sangay	"What China Could Learn from the Dalai Lama," *Washington Post*, July 4, 2011.
Didi Kirsten Tatlow	"Dalai Lama: No More 'Wolf in Monk's Robes'?," *New York Times*, June 27, 2013.
Tsering Woeser	"Checkpoint on the Road to Lhasa," *New Statesman*, October 18, 2012.

OPPOSING
VIEWPOINTS®
SERIES

CHAPTER 2

What Is the Impact of Chinese Rule in Tibet?

Chapter Preface

On March 10, 2009, the Dalai Lama, the spiritual and political leader of the Tibetan people, released a statement on the fiftieth anniversary of the 1959 Tibetan revolt against Chinese rule. In his message to the Tibetan people, the Dalai Lama reflected on the terrible consequences of the failed uprising and the dire hardships that the Tibetan people had faced since that time. "These fifty years have brought untold suffering and destruction to the land and people of Tibet," he wrote. "Even today, Tibetans in Tibet live in constant fear and the Chinese authorities remain constantly suspicious of them. Today, the religion, culture, and identity, which successive generations of Tibetans have considered more precious than their lives, are nearing extinction; in short, the Tibetan people are regarded like criminals deserving to be put to death."

The Dalai Lama's message presents one of the international community's main concerns about China's rule of Tibet: the preservation of the latter's rich cultural, linguistic, and religious heritage. In a 2012 report titled *60 Years of Chinese Misrule: Arguing Cultural Genocide in Tibet*, the International Campaign for Tibet summarized the impact of Chinese policies in the following words:

> The Chinese authorities have engaged in a consistent effort over 60-plus years to replace authentic, organic Tibetan culture with a state-approved and controlled version that comports with the ideological, political and economic objectives of the Chinese Communist Party. . . . This effort has been pursued through intentional policies that are designed to fundamentally alter Tibetan culture in a way that robs it of its essence and turns it into something that the Chinese authorities can manage.

These Chinese policies are so pervasive and systematic, the report concludes, that they should be considered a form of cultural genocide.

The concept of cultural genocide has emerged in recent years as a warning sign of much larger campaigns of ethnic violence and genocide. In many cases, the destruction of a group's culture is a precursor to mass atrocities and ethnic cleansing.

In his landmark 1944 book *Axis Rule in Occupied Europe*, Raphael Lemkin set out a definition of genocide as

> a coordinated plan of different actions aiming at the destruction of essential foundations of the life of national groups, with the aim of annihilating the groups themselves. The objects of such a plan would be the disintegration of the political and social institutions, of culture, language, national feelings, religion, and the economic existence of national groups, and the destruction of the personal security, liberty, health, dignity, and even the lives of individuals belonging to such groups. Genocide has two phases: one, destruction of the national pattern of the oppressed group; the other the imposition of the national pattern of the oppressor.

The international community's charge that China is perpetrating cultural genocide in Tibet is just one of the subjects discussed in the following chapter, which debates the impact of Chinese rule on Tibet.

> "Today, thanks to the efforts of the scientific community and the Chinese government, large regions in the Chang Tang and Tibet have been set aside as conservation areas."

China Is Leading Efforts to Preserve Tibet's Environment

George Schaller

George Schaller is a biologist, conservationist, and author. In the following viewpoint, he outlines the major environmental challenges facing the Tibetan Plateau, a high region of harsh wetlands and glaciers that has suffered severe degradation due to climate change and ill-considered government policies. Biologists and conservationists have been collaborating with Chinese academics and government officials to craft policies to mitigate these problems. Schaller and others have facilitated greater cooperation in resource management between Tibetan communities and the Chinese government, encouraged a return to traditional grazing patterns in the region, and put in place policies to protect the wildlife indigenous to the plateau. The Chinese government has also set aside large amounts of land as nature preserves and has created a far-reaching plan to educate the citizens of the Tibetan Plateau about conservation practices, Schaller argues.

As you read, consider the following questions:

1. What unique community of animals live in the Tibetan Plateau, according to Schaller?

2. As reported by the author, what percentage of glaciers on the Tibetan Plateau are retreating?

3. How many citizens of the Sanjiangyuan region will have to be educated on the basics of ecology and environmental protection, in Schaller's opinion?

Chang Tang. It is a hard name for the great northern plains of the Tibetan Plateau in China, a name that conjures visions of wild emptiness, silence, and desolation. Most of the Chang Tang lies above 14,500 feet, a land where icy winds howl and snow falls even in summer. Yet these harsh uplands support a unique community of large mammals including Tibetan antelope, or chiru; wild ass, or kiang; gazelle; wild yak; snow leopard; and Tibetan brown bear, to name a few.

The Chang Tang

I first went to the Chang Tang in 1985, attracted by its little-known wildlife and its remote vastness, an area as large as Italy and France combined. Once, in 2006, my Tibetan and Han Chinese colleagues and I traversed the northern part of the Chang Tang in winter, and for the first 1,000 miles—roughly the distance from New York to Chicago—we did not see anyone.

Yet in this era of global warming and expanding human populations, no place—not even the farthest reaches of Tibet—can escape profound change. Since first visiting Tibet more than a quarter-century ago, I have returned year after year, witnessing that transformation with my own eyes and listening to Tibetan nomads—with their herds of domestic yak, sheep, and goats—describe it. They say that weather is more erratic, sand storms more frequent and violent, and springs and wetlands are disappearing as the permafrost melts with warmer temperatures.

The Effects of Climate Change

Scientific investigations confirm this change. An estimated 95 percent of the thousands of glaciers on the Tibetan Plateau are retreating. Temperatures have been rising at 0.3 C (0.5 F) per decade since the 1970s, double the world average. The turf layer of the vast alpine meadow habitat in the eastern part of the Tibetan Plateau is drying and dying, its organic matter releasing a massive amount of carbon dioxide and methane, and drastically reducing livestock production.

These shifts in Tibet's climate are occurring as human population growth, development of roads and mines, economic changes in the lives of nomads, degradation of rangelands, poor livestock management, killing of wildlife, and other problems are threatening the Tibetan Plateau, one of the most imposing geographical features on earth. At 965,000 square miles, the plateau is almost as large as the contiguous United States west of the Mississippi, and roughly half of it lies above 15,000 feet. Its huge bulk has an influence on regulating weather patterns, such as the Asian monsoon, and its great rivers—fed, in part, by seasonal meltwater from 46,000 glaciers—provide water to 1.4 billion people in the lowlands of China and southern Asia.

Conservation Efforts

My colleagues and I had originally come to study wildlife, but we have been increasingly taken away from the pleasure of observing animals to mitigating conservation problems that threaten the ecological integrity of the region and imperil the lives of species and livelihoods of nomadic people. Today, thanks to the efforts of the scientific community and the Chinese government, large regions in the Chang Tang and Tibet have been set aside as conservation areas, and steps are being taken to reverse the degradation of the rangelands that are so vital to the region's residents and its ecology.

This conservation work in Tibet has taught me important lessons. One is that nothing in nature remains static, and may change rapidly. Another is that the simple word "conservation" implies far more than saving biodiversity. Solutions must be based on solid science, sound policy, and local support, drawing on the knowledge, interest, and participation of the area's communities.

Many Conservation Challenges

Such issues were far from my mind 27 years ago when I started research with my Chinese colleagues on the distinctive and little-known community of large mammals inhabiting the high Tibetan Plateau. The chiru, or Tibetan antelope—the males adorned with two-foot horns rising straight from the head—particularly intrigued me, as it migrated long distances and its travels defined the ecosystem. I also was drawn to the luminous grandeur of the chiru's homeland, the Chang Tang. To date, I have made 26 journeys there, spending a total of more than 3½ years.

In that time, my colleagues and I have confronted many conservation challenges, including a period during the 1990s when as many as 300,000 chiru were illegally slaughtered and the wool smuggled to Kashmir to be woven into expensive shahtoosh shawls and sold as fashion statements to the world's wealthy. Alerted to the slaughter, local governments sent out anti-poaching teams and confiscated guns, and we also publicized the killings internationally. Chiru numbers are slowly on the increase—about 150,000 are thought to exist today—thanks to greater awareness and better protection. But poaching continues; recently Nepal intercepted a shipment of 2,500 pounds of chiru wool, representing about 11,500 dead animals.

What Is Climate Change?

Climate describes the long-term meteorological conditions, or average weather, for a region of the Earth. Throughout Earth's history, there have been dramatic, cyclic changes in climatic weather patterns, . . . which describes changes in Earth's climate arising from alterations in its orbit around the sun, among other factors. The subsequent cycles of glacial advance and retreat occur on a scale of between 40,000 and 100,000 years. Within these larger cycles are shorter-duration warming and cooling trends that may last from 1,000 to 20,000 years, or less. Scientists estimate that approximately 10,000 years have elapsed since the end of the last ice age, and examination of physical and biological processes does show that there have been periods of global warming and cooling since the last glaciation ended.

Beginning in the 1970s, measurements of weather and climate trends raised concerns that global temperatures were rising, not in response to natural cyclic fluctuations, but rather in response to humans putting increasing amounts of greenhouse gases in the atmosphere.

"Global Warming," World of Earth Science.
Farmington Hills, MI: Gale, 2003.

Identifying the Challenges

Two problems, above all, now threaten the Tibetan plateau. The first is degradation of rangelands, the result of ill-advised government policies and a growing human population, which has tripled from roughly 1 million in 1950 to nearly 3 million today. Starting in the early 1990s, communal pastures were divided into household plots, turning nomads into small-time ranchers. The government encouraged and subsidized the

fencing of pastures and promoted maximum livestock production. Settled for much of the year in houses rather than in
moveable tents, households soon began to overgraze their
lands.

Half of the rangelands are now moderately degraded and
erosion is in places severe. The many fences also impede the
movements of chiru, kiang, Tibetan gazelles, and other animals. Some try to leap over or crawl under fences and become
entangled, left to slowly die. In 2005, the government initiated
a program entitled "ecological migration" to relieve pressure
on the rangelands by relocating many households into new
settlements, where they are given houses and an inadequate
monthly government subsidy. But such resettlement created
unanticipated social problems, such as continual idleness—
some of the affected Tibetans said they felt like "empty sacks
that can't stand up by themselves."

Finding Solutions

I collaborated with various organizations, including the Wildlife Conservation Society's China program, in trying to allevi-
ate conservation problems, such as the ones with chiru. Starting in the late 1990s, I became closely affiliated with the staff
and students of Peking University, especially after professor Lu
Zhi established the Center for Nature and Society and the
Shan Shui Conservation Center. We focused on promoting cooperation in resource management between Tibetan communities and the government, incorporating traditional Tibetan
knowledge and livestock management into conservation plans.
We have offered better fence designs and have encouraged a
return to the traditional communal grazing practices, which
give pastures time to recover.

Losing the "Water Tower"

The deterioration of rangelands is also being hastened by
rapid climate change. Chinese scientists monitoring 680 glaciers in Tibet have shown that nearly all are in retreat and that

many could disappear this century. China considers the eastern half of the Tibetan Plateau its "water tower," as the region is the source of the Yellow, Yangtze, Mekong, and Salween rivers. About 75 percent of the arable land in northern China depends on irrigation from rivers originating on the Tibetan Plateau. "To protect your rivers, first protect your mountains," the Chinese emperor Tao Tu Yu said 3,600 years ago.

The warming of the plateau has increasingly caused wetlands, ponds, and other surface waters to dry up. And the melting of permafrost, which covers about half of the Tibetan Plateau, is leading to a lowering of the water table and a loss of soil moisture. Tibet's Alpine meadow habitat is expected to more rapidly dry out, crack, and slump, with the exposed soil eroded by wind and precipitation, causing it to increasingly disappear. The Stipa grass on the Alpine steppe, a favored food of wild and domestic ungulates [grazers], is short-rooted and may die out in many places.

Preserving the Plateau

Recognizing the value of Tibet to the ecology of the entire country, the Chinese government has taken important steps to preserve large parts of the plateau. A sprawling area in Chang Tang was established as a nature reserve in 1993, and three contiguous reserves were added in the adjoining provinces of Xinjiang and Qinghai from 1996 to 2007, giving protection to about 174,000 square miles, an area larger than California. In 2000, the government established the 59,000-square-mile Sanjiangyuan Reserve—meaning Three-River-Headwaters—in Qinghai province, encompassing the headwaters of the Yangtze, Yellow, and Mekong. Such reserves will be vital as climate change forces species of plants and animals to adapt, move, or die.

In November 2011, China's State Council approved a farsighted, community-based program of ecological protection for the Sanjiangyuan region. My colleagues and I are now focusing our research and planning on Sanjiangyuan, contributing to the efforts of the provincial and national governments. Based on the awareness that their livelihoods depend on a healthy rangeland, a number of communities have set aside land for wildlife, are checking the condition of pastures, patrolling their land against intrusion by outsiders, and monitoring wildlife numbers and water levels in lakes and streams.

This imaginative new conservation model of giving management rights to communities is now being slowly expanded throughout the Sanjiangyuan region. It will mean that a core of people in every community—a total of perhaps 20,000 throughout the region—will have to be educated in the basics of ecology and trained in the details of monitoring and protecting their environment. It demonstrates how ideas generated by communities and a small and dedicated organization such as the Shan Shui Conservation Center can have a far-reaching impact on policy and society.

To achieve a harmonious balance of rangelands, wildlife, and livestock will require an immense effort by private and government organizations alike. But the opportunities in Tibet and Chang Tang are exciting, allowing us to address the conflicting demands of conservation, development, and the livelihood of the region's pastoral people—and not just in an area of modest size, but in a vast landscape larger than many countries.

The Role of Tibet's Spiritual Heritage

The spiritual strength of the many monasteries in the region is also needed in this ambitious effort. The world's religions have played far too small a role in the environmental movement. Tibetan Buddhism, with its respect and love for all living beings, is particularly responsive to conservation. Most communities on the Tibetan Plateau revere a nearby sacred mountain, and monasteries have sacred lands, creating a network of small protected areas over the landscape. We have already involved some monasteries in monitoring wildlife and in spreading the conservation message to surrounding communities, following the vision of the 12th Century Tibetan saint Milarepa:

Do if you like that which may seem sinful

But help living beings

Because that is truly pious work.

| *"Tibetans have completely lost . . . their once sacred, pristine environment . . . under Han Chinese occupation."*

China Is Destroying Tibet's Environment

Y.C. Dhardhowa

Y.C. Dhardhowa is a contributor to The Tibet Post International, *an online news service based in Dharamsala, India. In the following viewpoint, Dhardhowa contends that under Chinese occupation the Tibetan people have lost their once-pristine environment to harsh environmental practices. One of the most galling is the exploitation of Tibet's mineral, oil, and natural gas resources in the Himalayan region, which is having dire environmental consequences, the author argues. The Tibetan people have no opportunity to determine how their resources are utilized and are basically at the mercy of Chinese authorities, who have shown no consideration for the land, animals, or people of Tibet. There should be greater international condemnation of China's shameful actions, Dhardhowa maintains.*

As you read, consider the following questions:

1. How many mine beds, deposits, or mineralized sites have been discovered in the Tibet Autonomous Region up to 2011, according to Dhardhowa?

2. What is the estimated potential value of mineral resources in the Himalayan region, according to the author?

3. How many Tibetans does the author estimate have been killed or have died under Chinese occupation?

The one-sided policy [of China toward Tibet] has robbed the Tibetans of their basis for cultural identity; causing the loss of their language in their homeland and commerce in dealings with communist authority, their culture, and now they're facing a natural resource genocide. Tibetans have completely lost the right to independently practice their beloved Buddhism and adherence to their traditional way of life, they've lost their once sacred, pristine environment, and their confidence as a people, for they're truly treated as third class citizens in their own country under Han Chinese occupation.

A Shocking Population Shift

"There is evidence the Chinese people in Tibet are increasing month by month," the Tibetan spiritual leader His Holiness the Dalai Lama has told international communities on various occasions, calling the population shift a "form of cultural genocide"; [these] contented and confident people [are] causing Tibetan marginalization by mass migration, which will render his homeland's people an insignificant minority; a minority that can be basically overlooked and ignored, for the Han Chinese or authorities of the communist regime hold all the power; economic, military, financial and political.

The Han Chinese "reasoning" goes, that once Tibetans no longer exist as a distinct people, and their land is settled with a majority of Han Chinese, China will have "legitimized" their illegal occupation and annexation of Tibet that has a separate National Integration in the history of the world.

Genocide of Natural Resources

So far, over 3,000 mine beds, deposits or mineralised sites with as many as 102 types of minerals were discovered in the so-called Tibet Autonomous Region (TAR), Chinese official media have reported, quoting officials from the regional bureau of land and resources. What sweetness of words for the Han Chinese! When an occupying power exploits the resources of the occupied land at the expense of the original inhabitants, it builds itself on the ruins of what it has destroyed, and such theft of resources is obvious, even when the occupier tries to hide its actions behind noble principles. This malfeasance [misdeed] is made worse by claiming that the benefits in question are a financial gain for the communist regime. When such wrongdoing is compounded even further by acts of genocide against the Tibetan people, killing thousands and dispossessing hundreds of thousands in acts of ethnic cleansing, the situation is very serious indeed.

According to various news reports, the mineral resources in the Himalayan region have an estimated potential value up to 600 billion yuan (USD 100 billion [in 2011]). Among the variety of mineral reserves, Tibet is reported to have large chromium and cuprum (copper); far higher than other regions of mainland China. Twelve other mineral reserves rank among the top five across the whole country.

Reading this has truly incensed me, because it lays bare the motivations of the Chinese government for the world to see. Knowing about the genocide of the Tibetan people and their cultural identity, how can the world do so much business with this country [China], knowing what their government is doing? It boggles the mind. The Communist leaders are corrupt, they deplore freedom of speech, and they do not care for the people, the environment, nor the spiritual ties this land has to those who live there.

Mining and Its Environmental Consequences

Mining refers to the practice of removing valuable geological materials from the earth. Mining occurs worldwide. It is used to acquire fuel materials such as coal and uranium, minerals, metals, precious metals including gold, diamonds and other precious stones, and materials with industrial, agricultural, or other uses. . . .

In the modern era, the quest for raw and often mined materials drove colonialism and territorial expansion. In the United States, the discovery of gold deposits helped spur westward expansion and attract settlers to the American West. In Africa, mined materials were typically extracted in remote territories and using local labor, but the materials (and their associated wealth) were often sent back to the colonial powers in Europe. This practice established a precedent for mining that continues in the twenty-first century, mining companies based in industrialized nations operate and prosper from materials mined in developing regions. Local populations surrounding the mines not only provide most of a mine's labor force, they may be left with a disproportionate burden of environmental degradation from mining.

Global Issues in Context,
"Mining," 2013. www.gale.cengage.com.

A Devasting Environmental Policy

Imagine the damage to the environment their 21 highway project will cause. Imagine the damage to the land with all the aqueducts and other means of stealing Tibet's natural resources, particularly mineral water, and excuses they will come up with to not have to be responsible for what they are doing in their own country. It is no wonder no date has been set for their latest scheme. It should bring international condemnation to them for their blatant attempt to ravage Tibet and other holy places of their resources, particularly their water, and take the identity of their people away just for their own profit.

Legal or illegal? China has invited many companies and transnational oil giants, including BP [British Petroleum] and Shell to explore for oil and gas equivalents after realising that its own companies lacked the expertise to drill in a region known for its complex geology.

Regarding my past 25 years of watching this experiment on my homeland, I feel that Tibetans are unable to exercise their economic rights to determine how their resources are utilised. They live in an atmosphere of fear and intimidation where opposition to an unsuitable project such as hydrocarbon extraction would have dire consequences. Perhaps one of the most controversial Chinese plans to tap Tibetan resources to date is China's new water scheme, labelled the "big Western line".

Tibetan "Blood Diamonds"

Tibetan natural resources should be considered a similar issue to "blood diamonds", the term which refers to the conflict over criminally obtained diamonds [in Africa]; sold to finance serious violent acts, including genocide and human rights abuses. The blood diamond trade has been recognised as a global problem, with illegal organisations in a wide range of nations benefiting from the trade of these diamonds.

Tibet is a case in point. China's extraordinarily repressive human rights abuses against the Tibetan people, combined with its efforts to exploit Tibet on a colonial mode include policies such as capital punishment, the one-child policy, the social status of Tibetans, and lack of protections regarding freedom of press and religion. The Tibet natural resource trade plays a similar role and is a global problem, with dictator and communist states around the world in a wide range of nations benefiting from the trade of these resources, including Tibetan water.

In 1998, China signed the three covenants comprising the International Bill of Rights, but it is still far from implementing these domestically and in Tibet. Individual and collective rights abuses continue to challenge the Tibetan people in their daily lives and in the future survival of their unique cultural identity.

Over 1.2 million Tibetans have been killed or have died under Chinese occupation. The communist regime systematically destroyed the many-hundreds-of-years-old culture of Tibet, with only 8 monasteries out of 6259 surviving to 1976. Of 600,000 monks, 110,000 have been tortured or killed, about 250,000 have been forced to renounce their faith, and over 100,000 Tibetans, including His Holiness the 14th Dalai Lama, have been forced to leave their homeland.

*"Outsiders watching Tibet say that the
level of unrest there now is new, and
disturbing, . . . [and the increasing] immolations could be just the beginning
of a larger, accumulating outrage."*

China's Treatment of the Tibetan People Has Increased Self-Immolation Protests

Lois Farrow Parshley

Lois Farrow Parshley is an assistant editor at Foreign Policy. *In
the following viewpoint, she attributes the growing trend of self-
immolations among Tibetan monks and citizens to Chinese cultural and religious oppression. The self-immolations trace back
to the Beijing Olympics in 2008, an event that led Tibetan independence activists to demonstrate against Chinese rule. Embarrassed in front of the world, Chinese officials began to crack
down on traditional Tibetan practices and any antigovernment
activity. They also forced Tibetan people to give up their traditional nomadic lifestyle for settlements, which resulted in a loss
of cultural identity. Self-immolations are a reaction to China's
tightening regulations, and self-immolators regularly call for Tibetan independence before they commit the act.*

As you read, consider the following questions:

1. In what year did the Chinese military occupation of Tibet begin, according to Parshley?

2. What percentage of grievances get resolved by government officials under Chinese occupation, as reported by the author?

3. How many Tibetan nomads have been settled on reservations in the past five years, according to Parshley?

"Whenever they thought I was not telling the truth, the interrogator displayed a handcuff, an electric baton, and a handgun on the desk," Namgyal, a 37-year-old Tibetan monk, recalled to human rights workers. "[They] asked me: 'Which would you like to choose? Confession or tools?'" Namgyal, arrested in March of 2008 and accused of attempting to organize an anti-Chinese protest, was held for over a year without official charge.

During that time, he was tortured and beaten. At one point, he said, "I felt my body was split into pieces. The cuff went into my flesh. I felt I was going to die. I asked them to kill me." Then, he said, "They put me back on the floor. One of them pulled a handgun from a bag and said I should not close my eyes or I would reincarnate as a demon after I was shot dead. He pressed the gun onto my forehead and the gun clicked. Still I did not say anything."

Namgyal's treatment, not atypical for suspected Tibetan dissidents, is part of China's response to the growing attention activists there have received in the past several years, especially after a campaign of self-immolations among the area's monastics. As international media begins to cover the burnings—so far, *Time* reports 8 cases this year [2012] alone and the *Washington Post* says there have been 15 since March [2011]—the antecedents to this horrifying trend offer insight into a question that seems difficult to avoid: why would anyone choose to drink gasoline and then light him or herself on fire?

Sovereignty Debates

The high mountain plateau known as Tibet has been militarily occupied by China since 1951. The Chinese government regards Tibet as part of China, citing former Mongol rule of the area, and it exiled the Dalai Lama, Tibet's former ruler, in 1959. But many Tibetans argue that Tibet has always been an independent country. These competing claims for legitimate governance can at times escalate into a sort of culture war, playing out between the high mountains.

While China has had a presence in the region for the past 60 years, its codification of restrictions against traditional Tibetan practices are relatively new. Since a wave of demonstrations embarrassed the Chinese leadership around the time of the Beijing Olympics in 2008, when hundreds of Tibetans protested Chinese rule, prefecture-level regulations have been rolled out in breath-taking detail. While many of these regulations appear harmless or even positive, in aggregate they make for something darker. New "social security measures," for example, ostensibly provide small cash stipends to monks as an old age benefit. But the pay-outs are contingent on meeting a state-regulated standard of patriotism. As part of this new "good behavior" allowance, the Chinese government has informed Tibet's monks they will have no need to perform the religious services they used to be paid for. The price of being "supported" by the state, in this instance, is the effective prohibition of their religion.

Unresolved Grievances

For those with grievances against the state, China has a tradition of finding justice in the streets. In imperial times, people would travel to centers of power and petition officials directly, sometimes by standing in the roads, banging drums and kneel-

Tibetan Protests Against China

In 2001, the International Olympic Committee awarded the 2008 Summer Olympics to China. The Chinese government invested billions of dollars in preparing facilities for the games and even closed down polluting industries in a wide radius around the site of the games in Beijing to assure relatively clean air for international visitors. However, the games became a global flashpoint of controversy, in large part because of China's conflict with Tibet. On 10 March 2008, hundreds of Buddhist monks from monasteries in and near Lhasa, the capital of Tibet, marched to commemorate the anniversary of an uprising against China 49 years earlier. The march also protested the continued imprisonment of monks arrested in 2007 for protesting. Violence erupted during the March 2008 protests, with police attacking protesters, and several deaths were reported. Tibetans attacked ethnic Chinese Han neighborhoods.

The March 2008 protests were reportedly the strongest challenge to Chinese rule that Tibet has mounted in twenty years. Despite efforts to block press coverage of the protests, China was portrayed as an oppressor and human rights violator in many world media only months before the Olympics. In China and elsewhere in the world, some concerned Chinese people protested what they considered to be unfair media coverage of their country.

Global Issues in Context, "Tibet: Conflicts with China," 2013. www.gale.cengage.com.

ing before mandarins' carriages to call attention to their problem in person. Nowadays, petitioning is still practiced, in a way. Many governmental offices still have "Letters and Visits" divisions, where citizens can report their complaints, which are supposed to be passed on to the appropriate governmental division. But since the cases often get handed back to the local governments that created the trouble in the first place, it's perhaps not surprising that a recent survey reported only 2 percent of visitors had their issue resolved. Within this cultural context, Tibet's self-immolations could be considered an extension—albeit an extreme one—of a practice dating back hundreds of years.

A New Phase

Still, some outsiders watching Tibet say that the level of unrest there now is new, and disturbing. Steven Marshall, a Senior Advisor for the [U.S.] Congressional-Executive Commission on China, spent more than two decades researching human rights violations in Tibet. Marshall says that other new laws— which prohibit monks from traveling anywhere without explicit permission from the governments at both ends, and allow arrests for things as small as "reactionary" cell phone ring-tones—are likely to spark more protests. He believes this year's immolations could be just the beginning of a larger, accumulating outrage.

Marshall says that the self-immolaters are remarkably consistent in their call for independence. "Tibetan has two words for freedom," Marshall says. "One refers to political independence for a country, and the other means individual freedom, as in 'civil rights' in English." He says the demonstrators have used both words since the 2008 protests. "They are doing this because they've reached the end of their rope. They've tried everything else. Hundreds of monks are in prison and jails, or were picked up [by the police] and never heard from again."

A Disappearing Way of Life

Even non-monastic Tibetans are struggling with Chinese regulations. While a majority of the population has been nomadic for generations, the Chinese government has started to forcibly settle the herders into compact, fixed communities, effectively ending their traditional herding lifestyle. Over a million people have been settled onto these reservation-like plots over the last five years. For Tibetans, it's a loss of more than just a way of life—these nomadic groups are perceived to represent the essence of what it meant to be Tibetan. It's the end of the frontier, and in many ways, the sudden loss of a cultural trope every bit as central to Tibetan identity as were, for Americans, the idealized cowboys of the old west.

The Chinese government says these re-settlements make it easier to provide better services like education and health care. Life on the grasslands can be tough, and some Tibetans probably do desire an alternative, easier life, which had not before been possible. In these communities, Tibetans are given Chinese language lessons, and for a period of time after moving, a small living stipend.

But that's not always enough. "People are having a tough time. They gave up everything they have, but they haven't gained a way of life, a way of livelihood," says Marshall.

An Emerging Trend

This weekend [in mid-January 2012], after a monk identified as Nyage Sonamdrugyu set himself on fire, around 500 angry protesters forced police to relinquish his body, which they then carried through the streets of Gyumai, a town in Tibet. China's state-run Xinhua News Agency said that an investigation found Nyage burned himself after his "secret love affair with a local woman was discovered by the woman's husband."

Radio Free Asia said security in the area has been tightened.

"I don't know what's going to happen," Marshall told me before this latest series of self-immolations. If self-immolation were to become a larger trend, it could be very significant to Chinese internal dynamics. But to the 15 monks who were willing to burn in protest, the significance of their actions, and all they were willing to give up to be heard, was already plain.

> "What . . . triggered these recent protests in Tibet . . . wasn't so much top-down coercion by a one-party state as the promise and practices of inclusion into global modernity."

Globalization and Modernization Have Increased Self-Immolations in Tibet

Pankaj Mishra

Pankaj Mishra is an author and political commentator. In the following viewpoint, he argues that viewing the recent trend of self-immolations in Tibet as purely a matter of a protest against Chinese authoritarianism is not accurate. It should been regarded as a reaction to globalization and modernization—a clash between Tibet's traditional values of collective welfare, Buddhism, and environmental preservation and the Chinese-imposed values of economic and social individualism. He compares the conflict in Tibet with that in Tunisia, which exploded after self-immolation protests had set in motion the events of the Arab Spring. It is unfortunate, he contends, that the international community seems to be too distracted by its own economic and social ambitions to pay attention to the protests in Tibet.

Pankaj Mishra, "Tibet's Old Way of Life Is Slowly Dying," *The Guardian*, December 8, 2011. Copyright © 2011 by Guardian News & Media Ltd.

As you read, consider the following questions:

1. How many monks live at the Kirti monastery, according to Mishra?

2. What is the name of Tunisian vegetable vendor who set on fire and started the Arab Spring, as reported his author?

3. What American civil rights activist did Vietnamese monk Thich Nhat Hanh write to in the 1960s, according to Mishra?

In 2008, the Tibetan monastery of Kirti was a focal point for the anti-Chinese protests that consumed dozens of lives and led to the imprisonment of innumerable Tibetans. In March this year [2011], the third anniversary of the protests, a young Tibetan from the monastery doused his body with kerosene and set it on fire. Nearly a dozen young Tibetan men and women have immolated themselves since then.

Self-Immolation as Protest

Self-immolation is a radical form of protest for Tibetan monks, a violation of Buddhism's basic tenets of respect for all sentient lives. "Desperation" was the response from Kyabje Kirti Rinpoche, the 70-year-old exiled abbot of Kirti monastery, when I asked him last month [November 2011] to explain the recent spate of self-immolations. He described the repressive measures of local Chinese authorities: indiscriminate arrests; checkpoints on the roads; police camps inside monasteries; and the ideological re-education campaign in which the 2,500 monks at Kirti, confined to their cells, are forced to repeat such statements as "I oppose the Dalai clique" and "I love the Communist party".

The foremost Chinese commentator on Tibet, Wang Lixiong, has described how the Communist party's oversized bureaucratic machines in Tibet, which reflexively respond to

mass disaffection with heavy-handed measures, impair the
central government's ability to provide an imaginative solution to the Tibetan crisis. And Tibet seems, at first glance, an
instance of an unremittingly authoritarian and secular regime
pressing down on a docile religious population.

The Modern Tibet

But it is also true that, as a path-breaking study of the 2008
protests by the Beijing-based NGO [nongovernmental organi-
zation] Gongmeng law research centre (subsequently shut
down by the Chinese authorities) points out, "there is now a
new frame of reference for measuring reality" in Tibet. The
report asserts that it is no longer "a self-sustaining Tibet protected by the natural environment, but a realm which, whether
actively or passively, is intimately connected to all of China
and the rest of the world".

For some years now, Tibet has been part of the world's
fastest-growing and globalising economy—indeed Tibet,
helped by government investments and subsidies, has enjoyed
higher GDP [gross domestic product] growth than all of
China. There has been a general rise in living standards. Many
Tibetan regions have been transformed. A new "Tibetan aris-
tocracy" consisting of ethnic Tibetan party cadres and busi-
nessmen has come to the fore.

A Growing Income Inequality

Many Han Chinese may reasonably wonder why Tibetans, apparently showered with government largesse, are so ungrate-
ful. But as the Gongmeng report points out, "the assistance
and 'development' brought by the Han is often accompanied
by forced change and conflicts". The logic of development, for
instance, forces Tibetan nomads off their grasslands and brings
Han Chinese migrants into Tibet's cities. The unavailability of
jobs together with the undermining of Tibetan language has

led to a general feeling of disempowerment among the population. And rural-urban inequality has rapidly grown.

Cultural Identity

Of course, much of the Chinese population also suffers from the humiliation of being left behind by a few lucky rich. But as Wang Hui, one of China's leading independent thinkers, writes, the gaps of income and opportunity in minority areas are "closely connected with the difference in traditions, customs, language, and the position in the economic market that exists between ethnic groups".

The radical dissimilarity of *Weltanschauung* (worldview) is crucial here. One Tibetan interviewed by the Gongmeng researchers clarifies that "a Tibetan's prosperity is more about freedoms such as religious belief, a respect for people, a respect for life, the kind of prosperity you get from extending charity to others". Chinese-style modernisation has imposed alien values on Tibetans, forcing them to accept "development" and "consumption" as the last word.

The Effects of Globalization

The authors of the Gongmeng report sum it up: "When the land you're accustomed to living in, and the land of the culture you identify with, when the lifestyle and religiosity is suddenly changed into a 'modern city' that you no longer recognise; when you can no longer find work in your own land, and feel the unfairness of lack of opportunity, and when you realise that your core value systems are under attack, then the Tibetan people's panic and sense of crisis is not difficult to understand."

In this sense, Tibetans are akin to other uprooted and bewildered victims of globalisation and modernisation, such as the Indian villagers protesting against nuclear plants on their lands or the indigenous forest-dwelling peoples in central India resisting their dispossession by a nexus of mining corporations and governments.

The usual simple-minded oppositions between authoritarianism and democracy deployed in discussions of India and China are not of much use here. What these conflicts, cutting across differences in political systems, illustrate is a deeper clash: a powerful and aggressive ideology that upholds social and economic individualism against a traditionally grounded respect for collective welfare and the environment.

The Case of Tunisia

But what specific conditions triggered these recent protests in Tibet? The sociologist Béatrice Hibou offers a persuasive answer in her new book, *The Force of Obedience*, which, ostensibly about Tunisia, is also insightful about the psychologies of many other semi-globalised and unequal societies. Hibou describes how it wasn't so much top-down coercion by a one-party state as the promise and practices of inclusion into global modernity—the visible bonanza of GDP growth, the creation and co-optation of local elites, and the myth of an ever-imminent "economic miracle" that would lift all boats—that had generated a kind of "obedience" among the majority of the population.

For a long time, things seemed appealingly "stable" to foreign governments and investors. Tunisia had achieved a satisfactory macroeconomic equilibrium. It was slowly integrating into the world market. The widely advertised possibility that anyone could join the conspicuously consuming new middle class seemed to be defusing political anger among the disenfranchised. And then a poor vegetable vendor called Mohamed Bouazizi broke the spell, burning himself to death and igniting mini-revolutions across west Asia and north Africa.

Writing to [US civil rights leader] Martin Luther King about the dozens of Buddhist monks who immolated themselves in Vietnam in the 1960s, the Vietnamese monk Thich Nhat Hanh clarified that they "did not aim at the death of the oppressors, but only at a change in their policy". Events in the

Arab world following Bouazizi's death have confirmed the political efficacy of this extreme act of self-negation.

A Lack of International Concern

Still, Tibetan self-immolations cause more embarrassment than anxiety among Chinese authorities. As China increasingly appears as a saviour of many struggling economies, the world's conscience looks likely to be as little troubled in the future by Tibet as it is by [the Indian conflict area] Kashmir—British MPs [ministers of Parliament] had failed to even discuss the self-immolations until this week [mid-December 2011], and did so only after being pressed by the advocacy organisation Avaaz.

Most people may also be too distracted by the destruction of their own fantasies of easy wealth and consumption to notice a greater tragedy: that, as [British poet] Philip Larkin wrote in his poem *Nothing to Be Said*, "For nations vague as weed / For nomads among stones ... Life is slow dying".

"Even as desperate self-immolations among Tibetans . . . have increased in the past few years, there seem to be no signs whatsoever of China relenting on its cultural genocide there."

China Is Committing Cultural Genocide in Tibet

Rajiv Malhotra

Rajiv Malhotra is a physicist, businessman, philanthropist, author, and political and religious commentator. In the following viewpoint, he argues that China is committing cultural genocide in Tibet by facilitating the migration of Chinese citizens into Tibet, the secularization of sacred Buddhist sites, and the imposition of globalization, modernization, and economic individuation on Tibetan society. As a result, Tibetan culture is being significantly transformed. There are consequences to the Chinese occupation of Tibet for the United States as well, he adds: the United States should be concerned over China's exploitation of Tibet's natural resources and the establishment of critical trade routes through Tibet to Southeast Asia. To fight back, Tibetans can preserve their cultural and religious values and spark the independence movement by initiating the rise of a charismatic new leader in the vein of the Dalai Lama.

As you read, consider the following questions:

1. How many days did it take the Dalai Lama to make the journey across the Himalayas on foot in 1959, according to Malhotra?

2. What three Indian rivers originate in Tibet, as reported by the author?

3. In what country does the Karmapa, a Buddhist spiritual leader, remain in exile, according to Malhotra?

More than a half century ago, on March 10th, 1959, Tibetans revolted against the Chinese military occupation of Tibet that began in 1951. The revolt ended badly for the Tibetans, who suffered from a brutal Chinese crackdown. This caused the Dalai Lama, with the help of the CIA, to flee with his supporters to India. On March 31, 1959, after a grueling 15-day journey across the Himalayas on foot, the Dalai Lama escaped from the Chinese and crossed over to India along with 80,000 Tibetans. Ever since then, March 10th has been commemorated as Tibetan Uprising Day with worldwide protest marches to mobilize support for the Tibetan cause.

Even as desperate self-immolations among Tibetans still living in Tibet have increased in the past few years, there seem to be no signs whatsoever of China relenting on its cultural genocide there. At a time when movements like the Arab Spring get mainstream media attention, it is unfortunate that the struggle of the Tibetans seems to be slipping from public consciousness.

Why the World Ignores Tibet

Unlike the hot spots of the Middle East, Tibet lacks a natural resource like oil that powerful nations would fight over. The peaceful nature of the Tibetan struggle, unlike agitations in the Islamic world, has certainly generated goodwill for the Tibetans. But since they do not pose a security threat to the rest of the world as exporters of terror or nukes, it seems safe to simply look the other way. China's growing clout and persistence has gradually worn down the uprising, and Tibetans' support base among Western leaders is muted. Tragically, today's youth in the West seem generally less passionate to get involved than the youth of the 60s.

One wonders what lies in store for this movement. With the Dalai Lama aging, the Chinese know that time is on their side and are willing to wait it out. Without a new Tibetan leader of comparable charisma, they hope to accentuate internal clashes among rival Tibetan groups, offer carrots to some ambitious leaders, and use classic divide-and-conquer tactics to finish off the movement. Meanwhile, in Tibet, the land and sacred geography are being rapidly turned into secular tourist attractions under the ultimate control of the communists, and repopulated by the ethnic Han Chinese. Tibetan culture is becoming transformed by China, and "digested" into Mandarin identity.

U.S. and Indian Concerns

While this should be a concern for the entire world, India and the U.S. should worry the most. India's mightiest rivers (Brahmaputra, Ganga [Ganges] and Indus) all originate in Tibet, and China has started an ambitious project of rapidly building at least 20 hydroelectric dams in Tibet, each with the potential to divert water away from India and into China. Quenching China's thirst will come at the expense of India where droughts will result in many areas. I had predicted this scenario many years ago before it was fashionable to consider it, but only recently has this suddenly become a hot topic.

Tibet is also the military base for China's nuclear arsenal aimed at India, giving China the ability to reach India within minutes from launch. Tibet is the route through which the China-Pakistan links are transporting military and other goods

Fighting Culture Genocide in Tibet

The presence of elements of cultural genocide in Tibet is most urgently about the fate of the Tibetan people, but it is also a matter of global concern. The potential loss that this cultural destruction represents for humanity is significant and irreversible once it occurs. The international community must recognize the fact that this destruction is happening at the hands of a nation that seeks to become a great power with aspirations to shape global norms and institutions. Finally, there is growing evidence that such situations of cultural genocide represent a significant marker on the continuum toward mass atrocities, providing an important opportunity for prevention. The Tibetan people, from their highly vulnerable position under Chinese rule, have consistently taken every opportunity to assert their rights as the authentic arbiters of their own culture and to reject Chinese cultural hegemony in Tibet. Throughout Chinese Communist rule, the party-state has jailed, beaten, tortured and killed Tibetans with impunity for simple acts of standing up for their cultural identity.

International Campaign for Tibet,
"60 Years of Chinese Misrule:
Arguing Cultural Genocide in Tibet," 2012.

through modern highways, railroads and pipelines. This enables China to gain access to the Indian Ocean ports that are located in Pakistan, and Pakistan gets instant assistance from China in any conflict with India. Indeed, if Tibet could be neutral, autonomous and demilitarized, the India/Pakistan security situation would have the potential to be more easily resolved as a bilateral rather than trilateral one.

For the United States, China is its main rival and competitor in all spheres, a fact known and understood to both. While China has never hid its intentions, the U.S. has lacked a determined plan to address this. Tibet is China's path for the critical trade routes of the Indian Ocean, the Central Asian oil and gas reserves, and the rich ASEAN [Association of Southeast Asian Nations] countries to the south.

The U.S. Failure in Myanmar

As an example of its myopic foreign policy, the U.S. isolated Myanmar [formerly Burma] for many years on the grounds of human rights violations, which hurt mostly the poor people of Myanmar rather than the military junta. This played right into the hands of the Chinese. Had the improvement of human rights been the honest motive, the U.S. would have adopted similar measures against China where the human rights violations have been on a far larger scale. Myanmar was simply an easy target to get rid of American guilt and to show muscle. Thus China got a decade of monopoly in Myanmar which it used to solidify long term strategic control over Myanmar's resources and privileged access routes to the Indian Ocean. Tibet is again strategically located to make this possible.

The Tibetans themselves can also do much more than they have. For one thing, they must urgently initiate the rise of a new face on the world stage under the mentoring of the Dalai Lama. The Karmapa [a leader of Tibetan Buddhism] is one such young, charismatic leader with a deep grounding in Indo-Tibetan Buddhism and sharp intellect. Unfortunately, he remains largely confined in India. According to some sources, the Indian government is unsure if he is a Chinese plant—like a Manchurian Candidate. This matter needs to get urgently resolved [before] rather than after the Dalai Lama is gone from the scene. It is best to let the next generation of leadership become active internationally, and be tested in all respects while the Dalai Lama is able to mentor and watch over the transition.

We should not count on a change of heart among the next generation of Chinese. For China has done a good job in its education system to indoctrinate its youth to view Tibet as an integral part of China, and to demonize the independence movement as a conspiracy by hostile foreign powers with the top Tibetan leaders as co-conspirators.

The odds against Tibet are indeed heavy on such a loaded chessboard. But many other struggles also seemed hopeless in the past. I wish the Tibetan movement finds new champions among the youth of all countries.

Periodical and Internet Sources Bibliography

The following articles have been selected to supplement the diverse views presented in this chapter.

Soraya Beheshti	"Freedom Burning," Tibet Sun, February 9, 2013. www.tibetsun.com.
Sean Gallagher	"The Last Nomads of the Tibetan Plateau," Pulitzer Center on Crisis Reporting, October 25, 2012. http://pulitzercenter.org.
Hongxiang Huang	"Can Green and Red Coexist? How Tibet's Environmental Challenges Have Become Untouchable," *Tea Leaf Nation*, May 6, 2013. www.tealeafnation.com.
Andrew Jacobs	"In Self-Immolations by Tibetans, Signs of New Turmoil," *New York Times*, March 22, 2012.
Tom Lasseter	"100th Tibetan Self-Immolation Reported in a Protest China Can't Stop," McClatchy, February 13, 2013. www.mcclatchy.com.
Emily-Anne Owen	"Behind Self-Immolations, a Cultural Genocide?," Inter Press Service, June 22, 2012. www.ipsnews.net.
Gloria S. Riviera	"The Ultimate Protest: Women Self-Immolate in Tibet," *World Affairs Journal*, September–October 2012.
Brian Spegele	"Tibetan Self-Immolations in China Hit Grim Milestone," *Wall Street Journal*, February 14, 2013.
Didi Tang	"First Tibet 'Self-Immolation' Convictions in China, as Fiery Deaths Near 100," *Christian Science Monitor*, January 21, 2013.

OPPOSING
VIEWPOINTS®
SERIES

CHAPTER 3

How Should the US Engage Tibet?

Chapter Preface

In 1986 the Dalai Lama, the exiled spiritual and political leader of the Tibetan people, and a number of his supporters launched a campaign in the West that aimed to strengthen support for a self-governing Tibet. Known as the International Campaign, Tibetan exiles and supporters began to lobby the US Congress to force the Chinese government to ease up on repressive practices and allow more political autonomy in Tibet. A key concern was that China's rule of Tibet was resulting in a cultural genocide by systematically destroying the country's rich linguistic, religious, and cultural heritage.

The Dalai Lama played an integral role in the International Campaign. He traveled to the United States to give his first political speech in the United States on September 21, 1987. Speaking to the Congressional Human Rights Caucus, he proposed a five-point peace plan to resolve the Tibet issue: the transformation of all of Tibet into a peace zone; stopping the practice of settling large numbers of Chinese in Tibet; respect for the Tibetan people's fundamental human rights and democratic freedoms; the protection of Tibet's natural environment, including using the country as a nuclear dump waste site; and the start of good-faith negotiations between Tibetans and the Chinese government on improving relations and the future of Tibet.

The Dalai Lama also underscored Tibet's historical role and strategic position in Asia—a region of central importance to the United States. "Tibet's highly strategic position in the heart of Asia, separating the continent's great powers—India, China and the USSR [Union of Soviet Socialist Republics]— has throughout history endowed it with an essential role in the maintenance of peace and stability," he observed in his speech. "This is precisely why, in the past, Asia's empires went to great lengths to keep one another out of Tibet. Tibet's value as an independent buffer state was integral to the region's stability."

He also appealed to the rule of law. "China's aggression, condemned by virtually all nations of the free world, was a flagrant violation of international law. As China's military occupation of Tibet continues, the world should remember that though Tibetans have lost their freedom, under international law Tibet today is still an independent state under illegal occupation." The speech was very well-received and generated support from American officials.

The campaign was a success in the United States. Many members of the US Congress were alarmed to hear the extent of the crisis in Tibet and began to formulate policies to support Tibetan exiles and pressure the Chinese government to preserve Tibetan culture.

On December 22, 1987, US president Ronald Reagan signed the Foreign Relations Authorization Act into law. This broad piece of legislation contained some nonbinding agreements on Tibet: first, that the US government should make the Tibet issue a pressing priority, and second, that it should facilitate talks between China and Tibet.

In the ensuing years, the US government did not abandon its commitment to Tibet. Although it continued to recognize Tibet as part of China, the US government asserted its support for the lifting of martial law in Tibet, the release of political prisoners, the opening of the country to foreigners, respect for the press and international human rights organizations, and the call for discussions between Chinese officials and the Dalai Lama. The United States also established a cultural and educational exchange with Tibet, offered scholarships to Tibetan students, and funded radio broadcasts that aired in the Tibetan language.

On May 9, 2001, a new proposed piece of legislation, the Tibetan Policy Act of 2001, was introduced in the Senate and the House of Representatives. In September 2002 the main components of this bill were subsumed into the Foreign Relations Authorization Act. Known as The Tibetan Policy Act of 2002, the provision sets out US policy on human rights, religious and democratic freedom, economic development, and political prisoners in Tibet. It also created a special position in the US State Department, the Special Coordinator for Tibet Issues, to oversee US policy implementation and diplomacy in the region and to facilitate discussions between the Chinese and the Dalai Lama.

The Tibetan Policy Act is a landmark piece of legislation marking a new relationship between the United States and Tibet. The debate over the future of the Tibetan Policy Act is seen in the following chapter, which proposes various ways the United States can engage Tibet. Other viewpoints in the chapter contend that the United States should stop interfering in Chinese affairs and take more of a leadership role when it comes to protecting human rights in Tibet.

> "[Congress] should take a fresh look at how the nearly decade-old [Tibetan Policy] Act can be strengthened."

The US Congress Should Strengthen the Tibetan Policy Act

Richard Gere

Richard Gere is a Golden Globe–winning actor and the chairman of the board of directors of the International Campaign for Tibet. In the following viewpoint, taken from congressional testimony, he describes China's increasingly harsh treatment of Tibet and Burma (now Myanmar) in recent years and contends that the United States must do a better job in engaging China while acting in accordance with its own values on human rights and self-determination. Strengthening the Tibetan Policy Act is a key way to do this, Gere argues. The United States should facilitate more dialogue between China and Tibet; support bilingual education in Tibet; improve its advocacy for political prisoners; give more attention to economic development projects initiated by the Chinese in Tibet; and properly fund Tibetan programs.

Richard Gere, Statement at "Religious Freedom, Democracy, Human Rights in Asia: Status of Implementation of the Tibetan Policy Act, Block Burmese JADE Act, and North Korean Human Rights Act," House Foreign Affairs Committee, United States Congress, June 2, 2011.

As you read, consider the following questions:

1. When did the US Congress pass the Tibetan Policy Act, as stated by Gere?

2. What are the accomplishments of the Tibet Fulbright Program, according to the author?

3. At what age was the Panchen Lama and his family abducted by Chinese authorities, according to Gere?

As Chairman of the Board of the International Campaign for Tibet, I appreciate the opportunity to testify on an issue that challenges our moral compass and our ability to settle fundamental differences between peoples without resorting to violence. There are few international issues that have remained unresolved as long as Tibet has, nor one that has so intensely engaged the emotions of the American people. We care about Tibet. As Senator Daniel Patrick Moynihan once said, "The Chinese invasion of Tibet in 1949 does not become less criminal because it has remained in place over a long period of time. . . . The Chinese have been brutal and have made no bones about it and have made no apologies for it."

The Problem with China

The question of Tibet's incorporation into the People's Republic of China and the status of the Tibetans impacted by Chinese rule is an issue that continues to create obstacles in the U.S.-China relationship, and for good reason. China resolutely refuses to recognize the Tibetans' basic rights as defined not only by the Universal Declaration of Human Rights but also by the Chinese Constitution that contains clear protections for national minorities whether they are Uyghurs, Mongolians or Tibetans. I would like to note that more recently, we have begun to witness the same intensified persecutions against Chinese citizens also. Artists, writers, poets, activists, lawyers and free thinkers—even simple farmers have been aggressively pursued, in some cases "disappeared," imprisoned and even tortured—all outside of the framework of law. The vast apparatus of the People's Republic of China moves against any expression of free-thinking that is perceived as challenging the authority of the Communist Party—no matter how non-violent and benign—which sounds suspiciously like North Korea, Burma and any other authoritarian regime on the planet.

We should view the subjects of today's hearing—North Korea, Burma and Tibet—as case studies that are not dissimilar to failed systems where long-simmering tensions have erupted into violence elsewhere in the world. Cases where legitimate grievances are left unattended and fundamental freedoms are violently suppressed where the voice of the people is stifled and the rule of law fails to protect, chronically and systematically.

To quote Secretary [of State Hillary] Clinton, Beijing is on a "fool's errand" to think it is immune to change or that it can continue to suppress the will of its people to communicate freely as human beings on this small, interconnected planet.

What the United States Can Do

If the concept of the will of the people is meaningful to us at all—as many believe it should be—then we need to look very carefully at how we engage the People's Republic of China vis-a-vis Tibet. Here we can do and must do better.

We cannot engage the Chinese Government while forgetting our foundational principles of democracy and human rights. We cannot disconnect from people's quest for happiness—therein lies the stability and international security for the whole planet. The more we create policies driven by a sustainable, long-term commitment to universal values, the less vulnerable our societies will be to sudden—and often violent—shifts in global dynamics.

Recent events throughout the world remind us that policies designed to maintain the status quo—when the status quo is against the will of the people—have failed. This is morally wrong and puts us on the wrong side of history.

President [Barack] Obama has rightly championed the universality of human rights, and the Administration seems to have found a voice in discussing universal rights: "We support a set of universal rights. Those rights include free speech; the freedom of peaceful assembly; freedom of religion; equality for men and women under the rule of law; and the right to choose your own leaders." These rights are also the rights of Tibetans and Chinese, and as the U.S.-China relationship evolves, we must define policies with China that uphold the moral framework of who we are as a people and advance the strengths of our bilateral relationship.

The Role of Congress

Congress understands this imperative. For years, you wrestled with the annual debate over Most Favored Nations [MFN] trade status for China, weighing China's human rights record against the potential for U.S. business investment in China. I believe you eventually came down on the wrong side of this argument, granting China permanent MFN status, but in the debate, Congress wisely identified policies and resources to try to move China towards a more progressive political system, a system that would provide protections for the human and civil rights of its people and encourage the development of a vital civil society. In fact, if not for Congressional initiatives, I believe Tibet might not have survived, given the urgency and complexity of the U.S.-China relationship.

Now, I am no stranger to Capitol Hill. I know many of you well but many of you are new to this Committee and were not here for His Holiness the Dalai Lama's first congressional audience in 1987 or the Tibetan Policy Act in 2002, or the Congressional Gold Medal presentation in 2007 or the Committee's last hearing on Tibet in 2007.

I can tell you that you inherit an important legacy. Republican and Democratic Chairmen of this Committee and its Senate counterpart, Jesse Helms, Claiborne Pell, Ben Gilman and Tom Lantos led their colleagues in a strong bipartisan response to the outrages in Tibet. I ask you to carry this legacy on.

Why has Congress acted so deliberately to help save Tibet? In March 2008, Democratic Leader Nancy Pelosi visited Dharamsala as protests against Chinese misrule spread across the Tibetan plateau. She poignantly described the human rights situation in Tibet as "a challenge to the conscience of the world." Speaker John Boehner, standing next to the Dalai Lama in the Capitol rotunda said, "the people of Tibet have become well-acquainted with brutality and cruelty. . . . We will never forget the people of Tibet."

Recent Developments

But much has changed since the Committee's last hearing on Tibet.

First, the Chinese government has intensified its already restrictive policies that undermine Tibetan culture and religion, increasingly so since the 2008 uprisings in Tibet. Tibet remains largely sealed off to the outside world. Tibetans' language has been downgraded, their economic resources appropriated by the state and the people have very little freedom of expression. Hundreds of Tibetans, including monks and nuns, remain in prison for engaging in nonviolent dissent and are subjected to torture or 'reeducation.' The Chinese Communist Party has even gone so far as to say that the reincarnation of Tibetan lamas cannot be recognized without the permission of the Party. This is a distinct violation of a religious and cultural tradition that has been in place for a thousand years. This from a communist government that is by its own definition atheistic.

There are also now more Chinese than Tibetans living in Tibet's capital, Lhasa, while other areas remain under a form of military occupation. In Ngaba county, eastern Tibet, a young monk named Phuntsok recently set himself on fire in protest of the harsh reality Tibetans inside Tibet continue to endure. His death prompted prayers—not revolt—but the Chinese authorities fearing the spread of a jasmine-like revolution [referring to the revolution in Tunisia] in already restive Tibet—locked down Phuntsok's monastery; no food, no communication, no prayers—and relocated some 300 monks to unknown locations for enforced "patriotic reeducation."

Political Transition

Second, His Holiness the Dalai Lama has fully devolved his responsibilities in the Tibetan exile government to a democratically elected Prime Minister who will serve as the Tibetan people's head of government. This is the culmination of the Dalai Lama's decades-long effort to build a genuine democracy for his people. Today, this exile government does function democratically with three distinct branches, the Central Tibetan Administration, the Parliament in Exile and the Supreme Justice Commission.

The new popularly-elected prime minister, or *Kalon Tripa*, is Dr. Lobsang Sangay. This remarkable new leader was born a refugee in India. His parents, originally nomads, sold a cow to pay for his education. He seized the opportunity—provided by the United States Congress—to study in America under the Tibet Fulbright Program, which has brought more than 300 Tibetans to American universities since 1993. Lobsang Sangay earned his law degree from Harvard University and was serving as a Research Fellow at Harvard's East Asian Legal Studies

Program at the time of his election. He now returns to India to guide the Tibetan people through this unprecedented transition.

I urge the Committee to hear directly from Tibetan leaders who represent the views and priorities of their own people. His Holiness the Dalai Lama will be in Washington for 10 days in July [2011]. Lobsang Sangay will be here as well. Mr. Lodi Gyari, the Special Envoy of His Holiness the Dalai Lama, is a Washington resident.

Powerful China

Third, as China expands economically, it has assumed a far more self-confident posture. I imagine that the Committee and the Administration may be familiar with this dynamic in many areas such as currency, intellectual property, and the South China Sea. Anyone, anywhere who voices concern for China's policies in Tibet are met with shrill and dismissive attacks. China now includes Tibet as a "core issue" of sovereignty and territorial integrity—along with Hong Kong and Taiwan—effectively taking them off the table for discussion. Tibet has not been afforded the privileges of autonomy that Hong Kong enjoys under the 'one party, two systems' rubric although, ironically, the "17 point agreement" signed by the Chinese and Tibetan governments in 1951 was the first instance of this system. The agreement faltered and ultimately failed and was renounced by both sides following the 1959 escape of the Dalai Lama into exile.

The fact is that the cycle of uprising and repression will continue in Tibet unless China deals with the legitimate underlying grievances of the Tibetan people. This is as clear today as it was in 1959. His Holiness the Dalai Lama, who seeks a negotiated solution for Tibet based on the needs of both Tibetans and Chinese within the Constitution of the People's Republic of China, is facing a Chinese system that in practice pits Chinese interests against Tibetan interests and seeks assimilation rather than protection of Tibetan identity. It's a Chinese policy planned by technocrats in Beijing who are thousands of miles and thousands of years distanced from the Tibetan experience. Stability achieved through the will of the people, not through force or coercion is the answer for Tibet. The Dalai Lama is the strongest influence in the Tibetan psyche. Tibetans may live in the People's Republic of China, but they are not Chinese—not to themselves nor to the Han Chinese who treat them as third-class citizens. The inability to recognize or change this, which in context is a genuine civil rights issue, will never allow the Chinese to equitably resolve and prevent the unending cycle of repression, uprising, and more repression.

The Tibetan Policy Act

The Tibetan Policy Act is a cornerstone of the U.S. approach toward Tibet. I thank the preceding witness from the Administration for his testimony on implementation of the Act. I regret that the U.S. Special Coordinator for Tibetan Issues, Under Secretary for Democracy and Global Affairs Maria Otero, was not able to be here today. She has not yet publicly testified on Tibet. Undersecretary Otero is an expert on development among disadvantaged populations, among other things, and has much to bring to her Tibet portfolio. I urge the Committee to seek her input as the Committee gives further review to the Tibetan Policy Act.

Oversight of the Act is warranted. For example, Congress has directed the establishment of a U.S. consulate in Lhasa. Lhasa has been on the top of the State Department's priority list for consulates in China. The Committee should require that the Department not consent to another Chinese consulate in the U.S. until the Chinese agree to open one in Lhasa. This is an on-going issue but a rather important one that should be moved to the top of the priority list and frankly is, something I addressed in my previous testimony in front of this Committee.

Moving Dialogue Forward

A central tenet of the Tibetan Policy Act is to promote dialogue between Chinese officials and the Dalai Lama's envoys. There have been nine rounds of this dialogue since 2002. The most recent was in January 2010, now leaving the longest gap between rounds since the dialogue began. The dialogue has not led to a breakthrough, as each side basically remains at first principles. The Chinese see it only as regarding the personal future of the Dalai Lama while the Tibetans see it as addressing longstanding, legitimate grievances and the survival of six million Tibetans inside Tibet.

Under the Act, the State Department is required to report on the status of the dialogue. The report is not public, and last year's edition was late. I urge the Committee to ask that the report be made public, and recommend that the Committee hear from Lodi Gyari, the Special Envoy of His Holiness the Dalai Lama and the key Tibetan Representative in the dialogue, on ways in which the United States can move this dialogue forward.

Language Policy

The stated purpose of the Tibetan Policy Act is to "support the aspirations of the Tibetan people to safeguard their distinct identity." Language is a key factor in shaping identity, and Tibetan language is actively under threat in the People's Republic of China. Last year, Chinese authorities announced plans to restrict the use in schools of "minority" languages like Tibetan in favor of instruction in Mandarin. Tibetan school and college students protested against these plans. The scale of the protests across Tibet at a time of already intense political repression reflects the desperation of Tibetans about

131

the marginalization and erosion of their language, the bedrock of the Tibetan identity, religion and culture.

The Committee should urge the Administration to make bilingual education a central component in the U.S.-China education dialogue. The "100,000 Strong" educational exchange initiative should be broadened beyond just Mandarin so that American students can study in Tibet, East Turkestan and Inner Mongolia and learn their languages, and that students from those regions, not just Chinese students, can study in the U.S.

Political Prisoners

The Tibetan Policy Act calls for advocacy for political prisoners. The International Campaign for Tibet monitors the status of Tibetan political prisoners, as does the Congressional-Executive Commission on China. I encourage the Committee to avail itself of these resources, and to request regular briefings from the State Department on the status of its advocacy with their Chinese counterparts. No Tibetan political prisoner has been released into the care of the U.S. since the first term [2001–2005] of the George W. Bush Administration. This is clearly a result of the hardening of the Chinese position, the inadequacy of the U.S.-China human rights dialogue, and the failure to demonstrate a consistent human rights policy into the breadth of U.S. engagement with China.

Perhaps the most notable political prisoner is the 11th Panchen Lama, Gedhun Choekyi Nyima, possibly the second-most important religious leader in Tibet who was abducted at the age of 6 after being recognized by the Dalai Lama. The Panchen Lama and his family were then abducted by Chinese authorities. He has not been seen for 16 years. The Tibetan Policy Act requires that the U.S. Ambassador meet with him. I have been asked to provide an update on the Panchen Lama's whereabouts but redirect the question to the panel and ask, when was the last time such a request was made by the U.S.

Ambassador and what does the U.S. intelligence community have to say in regards to his the Panchen Lama's whereabouts?

More Human Rights Abuses in Tibet

Let me cite two other cases. Tenzin Delek Rinpoche, a highly respected senior lama from Eastern Tibet, was initially given a suspended death sentence in early 2002 on highly dubious charges of involvement in a series of bomb attacks on Chinese government targets. There are very strong grounds for claiming his confessions were extorted through torture amid suspicions that the real reasons for his incarceration were his popularity among both the local Chinese and Tibetan communities—the Chinese authorities regarded him as a challenge to their demand for absolute authority—and he was an active campaigner against corruption in local government. Despite the obvious risks, tens of thousands of people from his local area signed petitions this year calling for his release or retrial, and there are serious concerns for his health.

Karma Samdrup, a high-profile Tibetan businessman and philanthropist, who had previously been embraced by Chinese authorities. He was sentenced to 15 years in prison in June of last year [2010] on charges of "grave robbing" dating back over 10 years, for which he had already been investigated and cleared at the time. Karma Samdrup provided funding for an environmental NGO [nongovernmental organization] run by his two brothers in Eastern Tibet, and was imprisoned when his brothers challenged illegal poaching by police and government officials. His brothers were also consequently sentenced to prison or "re-education through labor"—one brother was sentenced to 5 years in prison on charges relating to an oblique reference to the Dalai Lama posted onto his environmental NGO's website. The imprisonment of the three brothers cast a profound chill across a globally critical environmental movement on the Tibetan plateau.

I would ask Congress to return to the days when every member who visits China raises a case of a political prisoner in a coordinated strategy with the end goal of their release. If the Chinese refuse to discuss the status of these cases, we need to attach some value to their decision.

Development Projects in Tibet

The Tibetan Policy Act also includes "Tibet Policy Principles" that govern U.S. support for development projects on the Tibetan plateau. The Tibet-Qinghai railway, completed in 2006, has facilitated an unprecedented wave of migration of Chinese laborers into Tibet, who have benefitted from the employment and income generation provided by the railroad—far more than local Tibetans. This railway gives merely a glimpse of the potential impact of the half dozen railway lines planned by the central government to link the Tibetan plateau with mainland China. They will open Tibet up to new levels of migration, tourism, and international trade, which of course, is not necessarily a bad thing but counter to Chinese propaganda, the Tibetans will not be the ones who "prosper".

Because of short sighted policies born in Beijing without proper Tibetan input, Tibet appears ill-prepared and ill-equipped to deal with these plans. This deserves much greater attention from the U.S. government. For example, the Committee should study how Hong Kong limits in-migration from mainland China. This can and should be a model for Tibet.

The Tibetan Policy Act requires that Tibetan language training be available to Foreign Service Officers. I understand that this is provided for.

How to Strengthen the Tibetan Policy Act

Many points about the Tibetan Policy Act are properly addressed to the Administration. But Congress can do its part. The Committee should take a fresh look at how the nearly decade-old Act can be strengthened. As a first step, I recom-

Religious Repression in Tibet

The government's respect for and protection of religious freedom in the TAR [Tibet Autonomous Region] and other Tibetan areas deteriorated markedly, with a substantial increase in official interference in religious practice, especially in Tibetan Buddhist monasteries and nunneries. Repression was severe throughout the year, but tightened further in the lead-up to and during politically sensitive and religious anniversaries and events. Official interference in the practice of Tibetan Buddhist religious traditions continued to generate profound grievances. An increasing number of Tibetans self-immolated during the year. The government routinely denigrated the Dalai Lama, whom most Tibetan Buddhists venerate as a spiritual leader, and blamed the "Dalai clique" and "other outside forces" for instigating the 83 self-immolations by Tibetan monks, nuns, and laypersons that reportedly occurred during the year. Chinese authorities often publicly associated Tibetan Buddhist monasteries with "separatism" and pro-independence activism, and characterized disagreement with religious policy as seditious behavior.

There were numerous reports of societal discrimination, including of Tibetans who encountered discrimination in employment, obtaining hotel accommodation, and in business transactions, but because Tibetan Buddhists' ethnic identity is closely linked with religion, it can be difficult to categorize incidents solely as examples of either purely ethnic or religious intolerance.

US State Department,
"International Religious Freedom Report for 2012," 2012.

mend you review, and re-approve, amendments that were adopted as part of the Foreign Relations Authorization Act,

H.R. 2410, which passed this Committee and the full House in 2009. I note that the companion measure, introduced by then-Ranking Member Ileana Ros-Lehtinen, contained the same Tibet provisions as the bill drafted by then-Chairman Howard Berman. This is a testament to the underlying bipartisan support for the Tibet issue.

These amendments would strengthen inter-agency coordination and encourage multilateral cooperation on the Tibet issue, authorize appropriated programs and achieve a U.S. consulate in Lhasa.

The Committee can also ensure that Tibet programs are properly funded. I know that budgets are tight, but U.S. government Tibet programs are as small as they are effective. For example, because of congressional initiative, the Tibetan language services of Radio Free Asia and the Voice of America broadcast information every day into Tibet. This is almost the only source of independent news available on the Tibetan plateau, and it works. When the Dalai Lama met President Obama in the White House in February 2010, monks in Amdo lit off fireworks to celebrate that the world's greatest democracy still cared for the plight of Tibet. How did they know the new President would be meeting with their revered spiritual leader? By listening to the Voice of America.

American aid helps hundreds of Tibetan refugees survive the dangerous crossing over the high Himalayas. We provide aid to Tibetans inside Tibet through grants to American NGOs that promote sustainable development, environmental conservation and cultural preservation on the Tibetan plateau. This is sensitive and often difficult work, and those who dedicate themselves to its success must navigate carefully with partners on the ground to advance Tibetan priorities within a Chinese system suspicious of outside interest. The office of U.S. Special Coordinator for Tibetan Issues ensures that congressional intent in its various legislative and policy expressions—including the Tibetan Policy Act—is understood and respected. With proper oversight, this Committee can ensure that the office of the Tibet Coordinator remains funded, staffed and accountable to law and congressional directive.

Concrete Measures

These are all examples of concrete measures that Congress takes to ensure the survival of the Tibetan people and their ancient, unique and sublime traditions while China continues to press with obvious advantage against them. The two-pronged approach authored in Congress—policy and programs—has advanced the American values of self-reliance, dialogue, democracy, freedom and most of all hope—in the heart of Asia. It has also served to institutionalize the Tibet issue within the long-term U.S.–China policy construct. I've seen the critical impact of congressionally appropriated funds for Tibetans. They are meaningful. With a vision for a positive outcome in Tibet, we can do more. There are hundreds of thousands of Americans who partner with Congress every day in supporting this cause. Once again, we can do more, however, we need to be more strategic.

With the world changing as quickly as it is, with the internal pressures that are mounting not only in the ethnic minority regions of China but within the core of Chinese society and in its largest cities, there is an extraordinary opportunity, now, to resolve the issue of Tibet. We at the International Campaign for Tibet have never given up on the belief that Tibet can be saved with nonviolent resolution.

With the right attention from the United States—the most critical force for Tibet—there can be a resolution—without bloodshed. But stability in exchange for human and civil rights becomes an untenable situation for any regime and is certainly untenable for the Chinese Communist Party in Tibet. John F. Kennedy once said, "Those who make peaceful revolution impossible make violent revolution inevitable."

Madame Chairman, Members of the Committee, we cannot be daunted by the steep incline in the road ahead. You have created much to build on and there are tangible steps going forward we must believe are possible.

I am grateful to you all and close with the hope that the Committee will find adequate time for discussions with His Holiness, His Representatives and Prime Minister-elect, Dr. Lobsang Sangay in July.

This is what I would like to leave you with. China is intensely focused on Tibet—for rational and irrational reasons—believing it can move quickly to checkmate. At the same time, there is, I'm certain, a genuine and heartfelt understanding among world leaders of what is at stake here. Most of them have met His Holiness—and while facing very serious Chinese pushback, recognize that the Dalai Lama's position—genuine autonomy *within* the People's Republic of China is attainable and win-win for all players involved.

| *"The [US] Department of State is aggressively implementing the provisions of the [Tibetan Policy] Act."*

The US Government Is Aggressively Implementing the Tibetan Policy Act

Daniel Baer

Daniel Baer is the deputy assistant secretary of the Bureau of Democracy, Human Rights, and Labor in the US State Department. In the following viewpoint, taken from congressional testimony, he asserts that the United States is vigorously implementing the goals of the Tibetan Policy Act and is actively working to encourage a substantive dialogue between the Chinese government and the Dalai Lama and supports policies that sustain Tibet's religious, linguistic, and cultural heritages. The Barack Obama administration believes that collaboration with nongovernmental organizations (NGOs) that work in Tibet and/or with Tibetan refugees are central to meeting these goals, Baer contends, adding that US diplomatic officials continue to pressure the Chinese government to ease up on draconian policies in Tibet and allow for the preservation of Tibet's unique religious and cultural traditions.

Daniel Baer, Testimony for "Religious Freedom, Democracy, Human Rights in Asia: Status of Implementation of the Tibetan Policy Act, Block Burmese JADE Act, and North Korean Human Rights Act," House Foreign Affairs Committee, United States Congress, June 2, 2011.

As you read, consider the following questions:

1. How much money was allocated in 2010 to support various services for Tibetan refugees in South Asia, according to Baer?

2. How much did the US Agency for International Development's India Mission allocate for a two-year program to support Tibetan settlements in India, Nepal, and Bhutan, as reported by the author?

3. How many times did undersecretary of state Maria Otero meet with the Dalai Lama from October 2009 to June 2011, according to Baer?

Thank you, Madam Chairwoman and members of the House Foreign Affairs Committee, for inviting me today. It's my pleasure to be able to testify today on religious freedom, democracy and human rights as embodied in the Tibetan Policy Act of 2002. On behalf of Under Secretary of State Maria Otero, the Administration's Special Coordinator for Tibetan Issues, I can tell you that the Department of State is aggressively implementing the provisions of the Act.

The Administration's goals are twofold: to promote a substantive dialogue between the Chinese Government and the Dalai Lama or his representatives, and to help sustain Tibet's unique religious, linguistic, and cultural heritages. The Administration at all levels—from the President, Secretary, Deputy Secretary, Under Secretary Otero, Assistant Secretaries [Kurt] Campbell and [Michael] Posner, to myself—has urged the Chinese Government to engage in a dialogue with the representatives of the Dalai Lama that will achieve results. We remind the Chinese government that the vast majority of Tibetans advocate non-violent solutions to Tibetan issues and genuine autonomy—not independence or sovereignty—in order to preserve Tibet's unique culture, religion and its fragile

environment. Regrettably, the Chinese government has not engaged in a substantive dialogue with the Tibetans since January 2010.

Promoting Dialogue

The U.S. Government believes that the Dalai Lama can be a
constructive partner for China as it deals with the challenge of
overcoming continuing tensions in Tibetan areas. The Dalai
Lama's views are widely reflected within Tibetan society, and
command the respect of the vast majority of Tibetans. His
consistent advocacy of non-violence is an important factor in
reaching an eventual lasting solution. China's engagement
with the Dalai Lama or his representatives to resolve problems
facing Tibetans is in the interests of the Chinese government
and the Tibetan people. We believe failure to address these
problems could lead to greater tensions inside China and
could be an impediment to China's social and economic development.

Assisting Refugees

Another critical avenue for implementing the Act is our support for non-governmental organizations that work in Tibet
and assist Tibetan refugees in the region. Both the State Department and the U.S. Agency for International Development
(AID) support cultural and linguistic preservation, sustainable
development and environmental preservation in Tibet and Tibetan majority areas, as well as Tibetan refugee communities
in other countries, through numerous programs. In addition,
the State Department's Bureau of Population, Refugees, and
Migration continues its long-standing support for Tibetan
refugees through ongoing support to non-governmental organizations as well as the United Nations High Commissioner
for Refugees (UNHCR). In fiscal year 2010, $3.5 million was
provided to support reception services, education, healthcare,
and water and sanitation for Tibetan refugees in South Asia,

Tibet and Human Rights

The authorities continued to repress Tibetans' right to enjoy and promote their own culture as well as their rights to freedom of religion, expression, peaceful association and assembly. Socioeconomic discrimination against ethnic Tibetans persisted unchecked. During the year, at least 83 ethnic Tibetan monks, nuns and lay people set themselves on fire, bringing the total number of self-immolations in Tibetan populated areas in China to at least 95 since February 2009.

• At least three men were sentenced to up to seven and a half years in prison in separate cases for passing on information about cases of self-immolation to overseas organizations and media.

Numerous people allegedly involved in anti-government protests were beaten, detained, subjected to enforced disappearance or sentenced following unfair trials. At least two people were believed to have died because of injuries sustained from police beatings.

Amnesty International, "Annual Report: China 2013," 2013.

including new arrivals from China. Under Secretary Otero recently visited our programs in India and Nepal where we assist Tibetan refugees, and where we are actively seeking ways to strengthen Tibetan refugee settlements.

The U.S. Agency for International Development's India Mission expects to issue an award for a new $2 million, two-year program to support Tibetan settlements in India, Nepal, and Bhutan in July 2011. The new program will support the development of organic agriculture for selected Tibetan settlements in India, Nepal, and Bhutan; and build a workforce among Tibetan youth remaining in the settlements. USAID anticipates the program will result in increased economic opportunities which will encourage youth to remain in the settlements, strengthen community ties, and preserve cultural and linguistic traditions.

The Human Rights Situation in Tibet

We are extremely concerned about the deteriorating human rights situation in China and in particular in the Tibet Autonomous Region and other Tibetan areas. Recent regulations restricting Tibetan language education, strict controls over the practice of Tibetan Buddhism and the arrests of prominent non-political Tibetans reflect the difficult human rights situation there today.

Religious restrictions in Tibetan areas have dramatically worsened in recent years. Discriminatory religious policies exacerbated tensions between Han Chinese and Tibetan Buddhists and triggered the 2008 riots that claimed the lives of Han and Tibetan civilians and police officers. Chinese authorities control Tibet's monasteries, including the number of monks and nuns and interfere in the process of recognizing reincarnate lamas. Monks and nuns are forced to attend regular political "patriotic education" sessions which sometimes include forced denunciations of the Dalai Lama. Reports state that as many as 300 monks were forcibly removed from Kirti again in April of this year [2011], and paramilitary forces still have the monastery on lockdown. To date, we have no further information about the welfare and whereabouts of those monks that were removed.

The effects of China's Tibet policies are well-documented in the separate Tibet sections of the State Department's 2010 International Religious Freedom Report and the 2010 Country Report on Human Rights Practices in China, released by Secretary [of State Hillary] Clinton on April 8 [2011]. Our reports state clearly that the Chinese government represses freedom of speech, religion, association and movement within Tibet and routinely commits serious human rights abuses including extrajudicial killings and detentions, arbitrary arrests and torture. Our reports also reference the forcible return of three Tibetans to China from Nepal in June 2010, the first confirmed case of forcible return of Tibetans from Nepal since 2003.

High-Level, Consistent Engagement

The Administration's engagement on human rights issues in Tibet is high-level and consistent. President Obama and Secretary Clinton have spoken on these points directly to Chinese officials many times, including to President Hu [Jintao of China] during his January 2011 visit to Washington. The President and Secretary Clinton met with the Dalai Lama in February 2010, and the Secretary raised Tibetan issues directly and at length during the 2010 and 2011 Strategic and Economic Dialogues with China. Undersecretary Otero has met with the Dalai Lama four times since October 2009, and with his special envoy, Lodi Gyari, nine times in the past twelve months. Other senior officials have engaged Mr. Gyari as well.

During the April 2011 Human Rights Dialogue in Beijing, Assistant Secretary Posner and I raised our concerns about China's counterproductive policies in Tibetan areas of China, reiterated our call for a resumption of dialogue, and raised specific cases. We were joined in that effort by then-Ambassador [Jon] Huntsman, who visited the Tibetan Autonomous Region in September 2010. The U.S. Mission in China has made visiting Tibetan areas and engaging on human rights and religious freedom in Tibetan areas a top priority. While in Beijing in April, we met with United Front Work Department, which handles Tibet policy for the Chinese Government, and pressed the Chinese to set a date with Lodi Gyari for the next round of talks. We also met with Minister Wang Zuo'an from the State Administration of Religious Affairs. Separately, we provided to Chinese authorities a comprehensive list of individuals from across China who have been arrested or are missing; that list included many Tibetans, including six cases that we specifically mentioned in our meetings.

Our goals—to promote a substantive dialogue between the Chinese Government and the representatives of the Dalai Lama, and to help sustain Tibet's unique religious, linguistic and cultural heritages—are designed to further the intent of the Tibetan Policy Act of 2002 and create a more stable and more prosperous Tibet where Chinese authorities recognize and foster internationally recognized human rights. In furtherance of our goals, we have, since 2005, made the establishment of a consulate in Lhasa a priority. We continue to press the Chinese government to answer our request, while we reiterate our long-standing interest in regular and comprehensive access to Tibetan areas for international diplomats, journalists and non-governmental organizations. The State Department offers Tibetan language courses at our Foreign Service Institute and our staff at Consulate General Chengdu includes Tibetan speaking staff. In addition, we are working to translate our human rights and religious freedom reports into the Tibetan language. These measures reflect the Administration's continuing commitment to fully and effectively implement the Act, so that Tibet's unique culture and environment are preserved and allowed to prosper in the 21st century.

> "There is so much more that the international community must do if Tibetans are to enjoy the freedoms so many of us take for granted."

The United States Should Do More to Support Tibet's Autonomy

Stephanie Brigden

Stephanie Brigden is the director of Free Tibet, a nonprofit organization that works for Tibetan independence. In the following viewpoint, she documents a number of human rights abuses facing Tibetans living under draconian Chinese rules. An increasing number of Tibetans have responded to Chinese repression by committing suicide by self-immolation. Chinese authorities have isolated Tibet from the international community, which makes it difficult to communicate what is happening in the country. It is imperative that the international community, including the United States, do more to secure autonomy and preserve human rights in Tibet.

As you read, consider the following questions:

1. According to Brigden, how many Tibetans from all walks of life had resorted to self-immolation as of December 2012?

2. What type of prison sentence can alleged collaborators of self-immolators receive, as reported by the author?

3. How many years does Brigden say that protester Jigme Dolma received as a prison sentence for throwing Buddhist writings in the air and calling for the release of political prisoners?

As I write, we have just received news of what we believe to be the 29th Tibetan in the past month to set fire to themselves in protest at Chinese rule in Tibet. By the time you read this, it is likely that more have made this extraordinary choice.

At Free Tibet we have seen protesters die from their injuries and survivors disappear by Chinese state authorities. It's hard to imagine how bad the circumstances must be for a person to decide that the most effective way they can make their views known is to wrap barbed wire around their body—so that burning clothes cannot be pulled off them—drink gasoline, pour it over themselves, light the fuel and be consumed by fire.

Tibetans can't vote, their petitions to government are ignored, protest of any kind is criminalized and, once imprisoned, most Tibetans are denied a lawyer.

Risking All to Protest

Without legal or political recourse to address their grievances, they risk their lives, their liberty and the safety of their families to protest China's occupation of Tibet. This goes some way to explain why more than 90 Tibetans from all walks of life have called for freedom by setting themselves on fire—all other avenues have proved futile. There are thousands more who have protested in other ways.

The Consequences of Protests

China has responded not by negotiating, but by perpetrating further violations of Tibetans' human rights in efforts to stamp out dissent, which is deemed a threat to "One China."

We have seen military and security forces descend in large numbers on places where self-immolations have taken place. Over much of the last year and a half, since a young monk called Phuntsog set fire to himself there, the Chinese military have lined the streets of the town of Ngaba; road blocks restricting people's movements. Free Tibet has received reports of security forces ransacking homes, beating people in their houses and in public in a show of force and intimidation of the community.

People suspected of being involved with those who have set fire to themselves are criminalized. Rewards—the equivalent of a generous annual salary—are on offer for information about collaborators, and anyone suspected of collaboration can expect to receive a prison sentence of up to 13 years.

Free Tibet has documented a number of incidents of collective punishment of communities where protests have taken place. Last month [November 2012], a public information broadcast on Tibetan television outlined, in great detail, collective punishment measures for communities where self-immolations take place: the families of those who set fire to themselves will have any state benefits removed, communities where protests take place will not receive investment for local projects for three years; government officials will be "removed."

Other Forms of Protest

Although protests by fire have captured the attention of the international media, there are other protests across Tibet that have not gained such coverage.

Thousands, from school children to the elderly, are engaging in peaceful protests. They have been shot at—some killed, many more wounded—by Chinese security forces. Over five days in January [2012], in three separate incidents, Free Tibet

© PoliticalCartoons.com/CagleCartoons.com.

received reports that five Tibetans were shot dead, many more wounded, when security forces opened fire on peaceful protesters. We believe those suspected of involvement in the protests have been rounded up and detained in the hundreds; scores have been disappeared; many have been tortured and some have died while in detention, most likely from the wounds they sustained during torture.

Others have acted alone. Jigme Dolma, a 17-year-old girl, was beaten and detained by security forces for throwing Buddhist writings in the air and calling for the release of political prisoners. Her protest lasted five minutes; her sentence, after having been disappeared for several months, is three years in prison.

Tibet Is Isolated

The rest of the world knows very little about the situation in Tibet because few places today, except perhaps North Korea, are so effectively cut off from the rest of the world.

Internet and mobile phone signals are routinely blocked, particularly in areas where protests take place. When they aren't blocked they are tightly monitored and Tibetans suspected of "sharing information" are regularly disappeared or detained and receive up to life imprisonment just for sending an e-mail. One Tibetan, who declined to be identified, recently told us: "I really don't have the courage to sacrifice my life with immolation but I can spend time in Chinese jail for passing on the truth."

Human rights monitors and international diplomats are refused entry to Tibet, and the international media are banned. The only journalists who have reported from Tibet over the last two years have done so by entering the country undercover, hidden in the back seats of cars. Even then, most only manage to film through a car window.

Meeting the Challenge

All these impediments make securing and verifying information an extremely dangerous job for anyone inside the country, and a constant challenge for organizations like Free Tibet.

Free Tibet ensures that governments do know what is happening in Tibet, despite China's best efforts to gloss over and conceal the truth. Sadly, many countries choose to turn a blind eye.

We welcome steps taken by the U.S.—for instance Ambassador to China Gary Locke's public statement urging Beijing to negotiate with the Tibetan people to address policy failures in Tibet—but there is so much more that the international community must do if Tibetans are to enjoy the freedoms so many of us take for granted.

> "China demands the United States . . .
> not to support Tibetan independence
> and . . . stop using the Tibet issue to
> interfere in China's internal relations."

China Protests US Comments on Tibet, Says "Disgusting"

Ben Blanchard

Ben Blanchard is a reporter for Reuters, a major news service. In the following viewpoint, he documents the Chinese response to comments by US special coordinator for Tibetan issues Maria Otero, who had blamed the increasing self-immolations in Tibet on harsh Chinese policies. China's Foreign Ministry called the accusations without merit and offensive, threatening to file a formal diplomatic complaint with Washington. Chinese Foreign Ministry spokesman Hong Lei argues that US officials should place the blame on the Dalai Lama and pro-independence forces who encourage the practice. In addition, the United States should stop interfering in China's internal relations and respect its sovereignty and territorial integrity, the author contends.

As you read, consider the following questions:

1. According to the author, how many Tibetans had resorted to self-immolation since 2009?

2. How many Tibetans died of injuries sustained during
   self-immolation, according to Blanchard?

3. When did the Dalai Lama go into exile, as reported by
   Blanchard?

China's Foreign Ministry lambasted the United States on
Friday for "disgusting" comments by a U.S. official on the
human rights situation in Tibet, saying it had prompted them
to file a formal diplomatic complaint with Washington.

Maria Otero, United States Special Coordinator for Tibetan Issues, said in a statement on Wednesday that tensions
in Tibetan areas, including self-immolations, had been exacerbated by tough Chinese policies and controls.

Chinese Foreign Ministry spokesman Hong Lei, using unusually harsh language, said the Tibet issue had nothing to do
with human rights, ethnicity or religion.

"It is an important issue of principle which relates to
China's unity and territorial integrity. China resolutely op-
poses any country or person using any means to interfere in
China's internal affairs," he told a daily news briefing.

Ninety-two Tibetans have set themselves on fire to protest
Chinese rule since 2009, with at least 75 dying from their injuries. The number of self-immolation cases have increased
this year, with 28 alone in November.

Hong repeated the official stance that Tibetans had en-
joyed unprecedented advances and rights under Communist
Party rule, blaming exiled spiritual leader and Nobel Peace
Prize winner the Dalai Lama for inciting the self-immolations.

"The relevant U.S. official issued a so-called statement and
did not condemn the anti-Chinese splittist conduct of the
Dalai Lama clique and Tibetan independence forces and actu-

ally attacked and rebuked China's important ethnic policies; it is totally confusing black with white and right with wrong," he said.

"It is sending a serious wrong message to Tibetan splittist forces and is utterly disgusting. China is extremely dissatisfied with this and resolutely opposes it. We have already made solemn representations with the U.S. side," Hong added.

"China demands the United States abide by its promises to recognize that Tibet is part of China, not to support Tibetan independence and respect China's sovereignty and territorial integrity, and stop using the Tibet issue to interfere in China's internal relations."

China has defended its iron-fisted rule in Tibet, saying the remote region suffered from dire poverty, brutal exploitation of serfs and economic stagnation until 1950 when Communist troops "peacefully liberated" it.

The Dalai Lama fled into exile in 1959 following a failed uprising against Chinese rule.

> "[Congress] should continue to fund the important programs that help Tibetan communities, both in exile and on the Tibetan plateau."

The US Congress and State Department Should Support Policies and Programs to Aid Tibet

Robert Menendez

Robert Menendez is the senior US senator from New Jersey and the chairman of the US Senate Foreign Relations Committee. In the following viewpoint, he expresses his concern over the increasing trend of self-immolation in Tibet, noting that it is one of most repressed and closed societies in the world because of China's draconian political, economic, and cultural policies. He contends that the US Congress should take a greater role in helping the Tibetan people gain autonomy and preserve their nation's cultural identity. Menendez proposes that the US Congress continue to fund key programs that help Tibetan communities; intensify efforts to improve access to Tibet for diplomatic and journalistic personnel; and facilitate greater dialogue between Tibetan and Chinese officials.

Robert Menendez, "Unrest in Tibet," Congressional Record, 113th Congress (2013–2014), United States Senate, March 18, 2013.

As you read, consider the following questions:

1. How many Tibetans does Menendez say have resorted to self-immolation between February 2009 and March 2013?

2. What did United Nations Human Rights Commissioner Navi Pillay state about Tibet in fall 2012, according to Menendez?

3. According to Navi Pillay, as cited by the author, how many outstanding requests for official visits to China by UN special rapporteurs are there?

I rise to express my concerns about the continuing unrest in Tibet and the tragic trend of Tibetan self-immolations. Since February 2009, more than 100 Tibetans have set themselves on fire. Many of the self-immolators have called out for the return of the Dalai Lama to Tibet and for China to acknowledge the basic human dignity of the Tibetan people.

Like so many others, I wish that Tibetans would not choose self-immolations, a horrific act, as a method of protest. I hope Tibetans will find other ways to express their grievances and despair and halt these self-destructive acts. At the same time, we must understand that these sorts of acts are indicative of the deep sense of frustration felt by the Tibetan people. This is not a conspiracy of "foreign forces" but indicative of the deep sense of hopelessness of a people denied their basic dignity.

Under the Chinese Constitution, "All ethnic groups in the People's Republic of China are equal. The state protects the lawful rights and interests of the minority nationalities and upholds and develops the relationship of equality, unity and mutual assistance among all of China's nationalities. Discrimination against and oppression of any nationality are prohibited. . . ."

The Situation in Tibet

Yet Tibet today is one of the most repressed and closed societies in the world, where merely talking on the phone can land you in jail. Support for the Dalai Lama can be prosecuted as an offense against the State. Tibetans are treated as second class citizens; their travel within and outside of Tibetan areas is highly restricted. Foreign diplomats and journalists are routinely denied access.

The American people and Congress have demonstrated an abiding interest in the culture, religion, and people of Tibet, as well as a deep respect for His Holiness the Dalai Lama. We see Tibet as an issue of fundamental justice and fairness, where the fundamental human rights of the Tibetan people, as embodied in the PRC's [People's Republic of China] own constitution, are not being respected; where their culture is being eroded; and where their land is being exploited.

So I believe that responsibility falls to us to help the Tibetan people in their efforts to preserve their culture and identity and have a say in their own affairs and to be able to exercise genuine autonomy within the PRC.

The Role of Congress

Let me offer some thoughts on how Congress can help.

First, we should continue to fund the important programs that help Tibetan communities, both in exile and on the Tibetan plateau. While these provide tangible humanitarian results, they also send a critical signal to the aggrieved Tibetan population that the United States hears their plea.

One measure with which I am familiar is the Tibetan language broadcasts of Radio Free Asia and the Voice of America. I cannot overstate the importance of these efforts to provide perhaps the only independent source of news to Tibetans who struggle under the heavy censorship regime.

Second, we should embrace the statement last fall by U.N. Human Rights Commissioner Navi Pillay on Tibet. She stated

Recent Protests in Tibet

Tibetan students in the Qinghai province protested on 26 November 2012 after a book was distributed that said the study of Tibetan language was devoid of value. Although exact details of the demonstration are unknown, as foreign media is barred from the Tibetan region, it was reported that twenty people were hospitalized after the event turned violent when police arrived. Four self-immolations also occurred across Tibet on 25 and 26 November; more than eighty people have set themselves on fire to protest Beijing rule since 2011, according to activists.

On 10 December 2012, thousands of people gathered at the United Nations headquarters in New York City to protest Chinese rule of Tibet. Consisting of mostly Tibetans, the demonstrators held signs with the names and photos of the dozens of people who have set themselves on fire in China in recent weeks to protest Chinese rule in Tibet.

On 13 February 2013, an ethnic Tibetan man set himself on fire in Nepal in protest of Chinese rule of Tibet. The man, dressed in the garb of a monk, was rushed to the hospital; he was still in critical condition in the days following the self-immolation. Nepal is currently home to about twenty thousand Tibetan refugees.

On 10 March 2013, marking the fifty-forth anniversary of the Tibetan rebellion against Chinese rule, Nepal arrested eighteen people accused of "anti-China activities."

Global Issues in Context, "Tibet: Conflicts with China," 2013. www.gale.cengage.com.

that "social stability in Tibet will never be achieved through heavy security measures and suppression of human rights." She called on Chinese authorities to adopt the recommendations of various U.N. bodies and to allow access to Tibet by independent international observers and media members, noting 12 outstanding requests for official visits to China by U.N. Special Rapporteurs on various human rights issues.

Improving Access to Tibet

Third, the State Department should continue to insist on access to Tibet by its personnel. We need independent and credible reporting on the true situation on the ground, and the Department should work with China to take steps to see that the principle of reciprocity is respected.

Fourth, I encourage the State Department and other government agencies to join in dialogue with China and with others in the region to address the deeper strategic aspects of the Tibet issue. Instability in Tibet is a factor in the broader question of social stability in the entire PRC. Peaceful resolution of the Tibet issue could go a long way in demonstrating to the world that China is indeed a responsible and constructive member of the community of nations. In turn, Beijing's growing influence in the Himalayan belt, especially Nepal, should be assessed in a broader dialogue with other nations in the region.

"It is critical that the U.S. take a leading role and engage actively ... on measures that could bring near-term improvements in the human rights situation in Tibet."

The United States Should Lead in Urging China to Stop Human Rights Violations in Tibet

Yeshe Choesang

Yeshe Choesang is a reporter for the news service The Tibet Post International. *In the following viewpoint, Choesang reports that several members of the US House of Representatives sent President Barack Obama a letter expressing strong concerns over human rights violations in Tibet. The letter also urges the president to take a greater role in finding a solution to the Tibet issue by engaging with the European Union, Canada, and United Kingdom to that end. The United States should be pressuring China to grant greater access to international officials and independent monitors in Tibet; review its policies regarding settlement of Han Chinese into Tibet and the forced settlement of Tibetan nomadic herders; eliminate strict regulations against peaceful assembly, religious expression and practice; and end the use of violence and torture against political protesters and political prisoners, maintains Choesang.*

As you read, consider the following questions:

1. When was the letter from US lawmakers dated, according to Choesang?

2. How many US House members signed the letter from US lawmakers, as reported by the author?

3. How many requests for official visits to Tibet by United Nations officials have been turned down by Chinese officials, according to Choesang?

Members of the U.S. House of Representatives have expressed strong concern over human rights violations in Tibet and said they have written to President Obama asking that the "United States take a leading role and engage actively with partner nations on measures that could bring near-term improvements in the human rights situation in Tibet."

The letter to U.S. president Barack Obama, dated December 20, 2012, was authored by Representatives Jim McGovern (D-MA) and Frank Wolf (R-VA) and signed by a total of 58 House Members of both parties.

Working to Help Tibet

Congressman McGovern said: "With the steep rise in self-immolations by Tibetans and the Chinese authorities' failure to address their legitimate grievances, the United States must lead efforts to resolve the crisis. We welcome recent statements by the State Department, the European Union, Canada and the United Kingdom, and in this letter we urge the President to work with these governments to address the human rights situation in Tibet. The recent statement by U.N. human rights chief Navi Pillay provides a critical road map toward that goal."

In their letter to President Obama, the members of the U.S. Congress said: "We write to strongly urge you to make Tibet one of your top priorities for U.S. advocacy, especially given the desperate protests occurring in Tibet this past year. It is critical that the U.S. take a leading role and engage actively with partner nations on measures that could bring near-term improvements in the human rights situation in Tibet. As you consider candidates to be the next Secretary of State, we urge you to nominate someone who will champion this issue.

"It has long been U.S. policy to promote dialogue without preconditions to advance a solution on Tibet and to press for respect for human rights and the preservation of Tibetan religion, language and cultural heritage.

The Tragedy of Self-Immolation

"Regrettably, the policies of the Chinese government towards the Tibetan people have only increased in their level of repression, their intrusion into all Tibetan institutions, most particularly religious and educational, and their denigration of Tibetan culture. These repressive conditions have led to the self-immolations and protests by Tibetans. As incidents of self-immolation increased in frequency, so have reports of mass gatherings of Tibetans to mourn and express solidarity with those who have undertaken these often mortal acts of protest. Continued crackdowns by Beijing threaten to escalate the situation.

"It is in this context that we welcome the strong November 2nd [2012] statement on Tibet by U.N. High Commissioner for Human Rights Navi Pillay. She cited "continuing allegations of violence against Tibetans seeking to exercise their fundamental human rights of freedom of expression, association and religion," and pointed to "reports of detentions and

The Human Rights Situation in Tibet

Chinese security forces maintain a heavy presence and the authorities continue to tightly restrict access and travel to Tibetan areas, particularly for journalists and foreign visitors. Tibetans suspected of being critical of political, religious, cultural, or economic state policies are systematically targeted on charges of "separatism." On June 18 [2012], a Sichuan province court sentenced senior Tibetan cleric, Yonten Gyatso, to seven years in prison for disseminating information about the situation in Tibet and contacting human rights organizations abroad.

Secret arrests and torture in custody remains widespread. In June, a 36-year-old Tibetan monk named Karwang died due to prolonged torture in police custody in Ganzi (Kardze in Tibetan). He had been arrested mid-May on suspicion of having put up posters calling for Tibetan independence.

Human Rights Watch, "World Report 2013: China," 2013.

disappearances, of excessive use of force against peaceful demonstrators, and curbs on the cultural rights of Tibetans."

New Measures on the Tibet Issue

"We believe Commissioner Pillay's statement requires stronger efforts on the part of the United States and the international community to press China to respect human rights in Tibet. It should serve as a clarion call for a new level of collaborative and coordinated pressure and engagement with the Chinese government on the Tibetan issue, including but not limited to allowing access by independent and impartial monitors to assess conditions on the ground, including the 12 outstanding requests for official visits by U.N. special rapporteurs; adoption by the Chinese government of policies recommended by U.N. special rapporteurs, such as suspension and review of Chinese policies and incentives that promote the settlement of mainland Chinese into Tibet; the suspension of non-voluntary resettlement of Tibetan nomadic herders; an independent inquiry into alleged excessive use of force against peaceful demonstrators of 2008, and allegations of torture and ill-treatment against those arrested and detained; lifting restrictions on media access to the region; respect for Tibetans' rights to peaceful assembly, expression and religious practice, and the release of anyone detained for exercising those rights; and renewed engagement in dialogue with the Dalai Lama or his representatives without preconditions.

"The Chinese government appears to believe that by sealing off Tibet, international interest and concern will diminish. It will not. We were therefore pleased to see the recent statements by Special Coordinator for Tibetan Issues Under Secretary Maria Otero and by Assistant Secretary of State for Democracy, Human Rights and Labor Michael Posner expressing U.S. concern over the increasing frequency of self-immolations by Tibetans and rejection of the continuing violence by Chinese authorities in Tibetan areas. But much more must be done.

"We urge you, Mr. President, to take a leading role in support of Commissioner Pillay's statement and actively engage partner nations on measures that could bring near-term improvements in the human rights situation in Tibet and serve to de-escalate rising tensions brought about by hard-line and destructive Chinese policies and actions. In addition, continued attention must be paid to promoting dialogue between Chinese officials and Tibetan leaders in order to achieve a negotiated solution to the problems afflicting Tibet and the Tibetan people.

"We have the moral obligation to speak out for the Tibetan people and confront China about these abuses, to convey the aspirations for change that are being expressed so desperately by the Tibetan people directly to those who have the responsibility to heed Tibetans' demands for change, respect and basic dignity. We ask that you make this a top priority and lead the way."

Periodical and Internet Sources Bibliography

The following articles have been selected to supplement the diverse views presented in this chapter.

Agence France-Presse	"China's Hu Warns US on Tibet, Taiwan," January 20, 2011. www.afp.com.
Carey L. Biron	"Morality Versus Strategy in US Tibet Policy," Inter Press Service, May 4, 2012. www.ipsnews .net.
Ellen Bork	"Obama's Timidity on Tibet," *Wall Street Journal*, August 19, 2010.
Ellen Bork	"The Trouble with Tibet," *New Republic*, February 19, 2011.
Eleanor Byrne-Rosengren	"Rights Group: Obama Must Turn Up the Heat on Tibet," CNN.com, June 6, 2013.
The Economist	"Tibet, China, and America: Toward the Light?," July 19, 2011.
Richard Finney	"Can the World Help Tibet?," Radio Free Asia, August 10, 2012. www.rfa.org.
Frida Ghitis	"Tibetans' Cries for Help," CNN.com, March 29, 2012.
Christina Larson	"Tibet Is No Shangri-La," *Foreign Policy*, February 15, 2012.
Thomas Lifson	"Obama's Tibet Two Step," *American Thinker*, July 17, 2011.
James Rupert	"US Urges China to Ease Tibet Policy After Nun's Immolation," *Bloomberg Businessweek*, October 20, 2011.

CHAPTER 4

What Is the Best Way to Encourage Political Change in Tibet?

Chapter Preface

On June 10, 1963, journalist Malcolm Brown took a shocking photograph of a South Vietnamese Buddhist monk on fire in the middle of a busy Saigon intersection. The gruesome suicide was part of a coordinated protest against South Vietnam's systematic religious, social, and economic discrimination against Buddhists; in particular recent bans on Buddhist ceremonies and public expressions. Buddhist monks were at the forefront of the protests, which called for religious equality and freedom of religious expression. On that June day, hundreds of monks and nuns led a procession through the bustling capital city of Saigon to a crowded intersection, where a sixty-five-year-old Buddhist monk, Thich Quang Duc, sat down on a cushion while another monk poured gasoline over him. Passersby and press gasped as Quang Duc took out a lighter and set himself on fire.

In his 1965 book *The Making of a Quagmire*, renowned American journalist David Halberstam described the grisly spectacle. "Flames were coming from a human being; his body was slowly withering and shriveling up, his head blackening and charring," he wrote. "In the air was the smell of burning flesh; human beings burn surprisingly quickly. Behind me I could hear the sobbing of the Vietnamese who were now gathering. I was too shocked to cry, too confused to take notes or questions, too bewildered to even think. . . . As he burned, he never moved a muscle, never uttered a sound, his outward composure in sharp contrast to the wailing people around him."

Brown's photo of the horrific event was published in newspapers around the world. It captures the scene that Halberstam vividly describes: Quang Duc's eerie calm in the face of death and the resolve of his fellow Buddhist monks who surrounded him and prevented authorities from reaching the scene to extinguish the blaze. The photo would go on to become the World Press Photo of 1963.

Quang Duc's self-immolation was recognized as a political protest and garnered support for his aims from around the world. The South Vietnamese government quickly realized that the situation was becoming untenable. On June 16, 1963, an agreement, known as the Joint Communiqué, was signed by government and Buddhist officials to address many of the outstanding grievances raised by the Buddhist community. The success of Quang Duc's protest in forcing South Vietnamese officials to finally address Buddhist demands has since led other desperate protesters to turn to the horrific practice of self-immolation.

Most notably, self-immolation has been used in Tibet as a way to spur political change. Since March 2011, more than one hundred Tibetans have set themselves on fire inside Tibet as a protest against Chinese policies. A number of self-immolations have also occurred outside of Tibet. As in the case of Quang Duc, the act of self-immolation remains a shocking act of self-sacrifice and draws worldwide attention to the grievances of the Tibetan people. However, as there has been no significant change in Chinese policy, many commentators are beginning to question the efficacy of such grisly acts to force political change in Tibet.

The issue of self-immolation as a political protest is just one issue examined in the following chapter, which debates the best ways to encourage political change in Tibet.

"The UK government should coordinate its efforts with other like-minded countries and call on the Chinese government to review [its] policies towards Tibetans."

The International Community Should Apply Coordinated Political Pressure to Help Tibet

Bianca Jagger

Bianca Jagger, the former wife of Rolling Stone frontman Mick Jagger, is a political activist and the founder of the Bianca Jagger Human Rights Foundation. In the following viewpoint, she appeals to the international community, particularly the United Kingdom and the United States, to support the Tibetan people in their struggle for independence against China. Jagger offers an overview of the human rights abuses and cultural genocide suffered by the Tibetan people under Chinese occupation, which has resulted in a growing wave of self-immolations as a desperate protest. She urges the international community to press the Chinese government to review its policies toward Tibet and allow the entry of human rights monitors, engage in regular dialogue with the Dalai Lama and other leaders of the Tibetan government-in-exile, and expand programs that assist Tibetan refugees and activists.

As you read, consider the following questions:

1. What award did the Dalai Lama receive in May 2012, as reported by Jagger?

2. Why is Tibet known as the earth's 'Third Pole,' as described by the author?

3. What commitment did President Barack Obama make on January 19, 2011, according to Jagger?

His Holiness the Dalai Lama is in London today [May 14, 2012] to receive the Templeton Prize in recognition of his outstanding achievements and spiritual wisdom.

Tibet has a long-standing connection to Britain. Prior to the Chinese invasion in 1949–50, Britain was the only country to formally recognize Tibet as an independent nation. British representatives were stationed in [Tibet's capital city] Lhasa from 1904 to 1947 to liaise with the Tibetan government. In 1949 the newly-victorious leader of the China Communist Party, Mao Zedong, announced over the radio waves his intention to "liberate" Tibet from this "foreign imperialism."

A Systematic Oppression

Over the past 60 years, Tibet has been anything but "liberated" by the Chinese Communist Party.

On the 10th of May I delivered two reports to 10 Downing Street [headquarters of the British government]. The reports, by the Society for Threatened People and the International Campaign for Tibet, document the devastating impact of Chinese Communist Party rule in Tibet.

I appealed to Prime Minister David Cameron to support the Tibetans at this critical time in their struggle.

In recent months we have seen harrowing images and footage of Tibetans who have set fire to themselves as a form of protest. Since February, 2009, 35 Tibetans have sacrificed themselves, in an act of desperation, which emerges from the anguish of oppression. Tibetans who have self-immolated include monks, nuns, a 19-year old female student, a widowed mother of four, and a Tibetan reincarnated lama in his forties.

A Growing Wave

This is one of the most significant waves of self-immolation for the past 60 years, eclipsing the number of self-immolation protests by Vietnamese monks, those associated with the Vietnam War and the pro-democracy movement in South Korea.

The Vietnamese Buddhist monk Thich Nhat Hanh has observed, "To burn oneself by fire is to prove that what one is saying is of the utmost importance."

Although we do not know the last words of all the Tibetans who have poured kerosene over themselves and lit a match, we do know that most have died offering prayers for the Dalai Lama to return home, and for freedom in Tibet.

It Is Time to Act

It is time for us to listen to what Tibetans inside Tibet are saying. It is time for the international community to listen to them and to act.

Over the past four years, the Chinese government has engaged in a comprehensive cover-up of the torture, disappearances and killings that have taken place across Tibet. They have engaged upon a virulent propaganda offensive against the Dalai Lama.

On the international stage, Beijing has subverted and politicized international forums where its human rights record has been challenged and refused to answer legitimate questions from governments about the use of lethal force against unarmed protestors, or the welfare of individual detainees.

Universally Recognized Human Rights

The Universal Declaration of Human Rights lists the rights due to every human being. These are the rights to: life; liberty and security of person; protection against slavery; protection against torture and cruel and inhuman punishment; recognition as a person before the law; equal protection of the law; access to legal remedies for violations of rights; protection against arbitrary arrest, detention or exile; an independent and impartial judiciary, presumption of innocence; protection against ex post facto laws; protection of privacy, family, and home; freedom of movement and residence; seek asylum from persecution; nationality; marry and found a family; own property; freedom of thought, conscience, and religion; freedom of opinion, expression, and the press; freedom of assembly and association; political participation; social security; work under favorable conditions; free trade unions; rest and leisure; food, clothing, and housing; health care and social services; special protections for children; education; participation in cultural life; and a social and international order needed to realize these rights.

Global Issues in Context,
"Human Rights," 2013. www.gale.cengage.com.

A Cultural Genocide

Over the past 60 years, the Chinese government has instituted increasingly hardline policies that undermine Tibetan culture and religion. The Tibetan people have been denied freedom of expression. Their language has been downgraded. And their economic resources have been misappropriated by the Chinese state, with increasing numbers of Chinese migrants moving to the Tibetan plateau.

China's economic strategies are literally re-shaping the Tibetan landscape and endangering the fragile ecosystem of the world's largest and highest altitude plateau. The survival of one of the world's only remaining systems of sustainable pastoralism [herders] is under threat, as nomads are being displaced from their ancestral lands and settled into remote concrete encampments under an urbanization drive.

Why Tibet Matters

Why should Tibet matter? It matters because of the terrible suffering of its people, and because of the need for this ancient religion and the Tibetan cultural identity to survive. This is a culture based on the concepts of wisdom, compassion and inter-dependence. These are valuable teachings for the Tibetan people, and for the world.

The survival of Tibet is not just a moral issue. The country is situated in a strategic geopolitical position, between two nuclear giants, India and China. The future of Tibet is tied to Asian and international security.

Tibet is known as the earth's 'Third Pole', with the largest supply of fresh water [in the form of glaciers] in the world outside the two Poles. Most of Asia's major rivers have their sources in Tibet, meaning that development policies, damming and land degradation in Tibet can affect hundreds of millions of people elsewhere. China cannot claim that Tibet is their 'internal affair.'

This is a critical year for China. Divisions in the Chinese Communist Party have been exposed amidst a new clamor for genuine reform. At this historic juncture the international community should be actively engaged in finding a solution to the crisis in Tibet.

What Britain Should Do

In our letter to David Cameron, we urged him to lead a multilateral effort in support of Tibet. The UK government should coordinate its efforts with other like-minded countries and call on the Chinese government to review the policies towards Tibetans that are the root cause of the self-immolations, the ongoing tensions and unrest, and which are threatening the unique culture, religion, and identity of the Tibetan people. The UK government, together with the European Commission should maintain and where possible expand targeted programmatic assistance for Tibetans including support for sustainable, culturally appropriate development assistance to Tibetan communities; educational and cultural exchange programs targeted to Tibetans both in Tibet and in exile.

Amnesty [International] has also requested that the Chinese government allow independent monitors, for instance, the UN Special Rapporteur on extrajudicial, summary or arbitrary executions, into the country.

The international community should engage in regular dialogue with Tibetan representatives, including the Dalai Lama and his representatives, and Lobsang Sangay, the new Tibetan Prime Minister in exile, to address the immediate crisis in Tibet.

What the United States Should Do

I urge President [Barack] Obama to take concrete steps to demonstrate his commitment to the fundamental human rights of the Tibetan people, and stand by his words of January 19th, 2011, when he professed 'America's fundamental commitment to the universal rights of all people. That includes basic human rights like freedom of speech, of the press, of assembly, of association and demonstration, and of religion—rights that are recognized in the Chinese constitution. . . . Even as we, the United States, recognize that Tibet is part of the People's Republic of China, the United States continues to support further dialogue between the government of China and the representatives of the Dalai Lama to resolve concerns and differences, including the preservation of the religious and cultural identity of the Tibetan people.'

The religious and cultural identity of the Tibetan people is under threat in Tibet today. The Tibetans are standing up to the vast and expanding power of the Chinese state with non-violent resistance through religious practice, song, literature, and even self-immolation. They are struggling to preserve their religion and cultural identity. As a consequence they are subjected to imprisonment, torture, deprivation and worse. Yet they persevere. Their bravery should serve as a call to action. I call upon the international community to act now on behalf of Tibet. Time is running out. The very survival of the Tibetan people hangs in the balance.

> *"We need a global campaign to counter [Chinese propaganda about Tibet], and a boycott has the best chance of sparking it."*

A Global Boycott on Chinese Goods Will Spur Political Change in Tibet

Jonathan Zimmerman

Jonathan Zimmerman is an educator and author. In the following viewpoint, he contends that a new strategy is needed to force China to pay attention to the protests of the international community regarding its harsh treatment of Tibet: a worldwide boycott on Chinese goods. Such a boycott has its obvious limitations, because so many products are made in China that it would be impossible to impose a total boycott. Such a move would have much symbolic importance, he argues, and would succeed in focusing global attention on the reality of the Tibet issue. It is imperative that myths perpetrated about the ignorance of Tibetans and the good China has done for Tibet are exposed and countered with the truth about what the Tibetan people have experienced, Zimmerman maintains.

As you read, consider the following questions:

1. When did Chinese authorities declare martial law in Lhasa, Tibet, according to Zimmerman?

2. What country's activists were the instigators of a 2008 proposed boycott on Chinese goods, as reported by the author?

3. How many Americans does Zimmerman say were detained by Chinese officials after a US surveillance plane was downed in 2001?

In the early 1980s, as a Peace Corps volunteer in Nepal, I wore a "Free Tibet" patch on my backpack. Two summers ago, when I returned to my old Nepalese village with my 16-year-old daughter, she affixed the same words to her water bottle.

And still, Tibet is not free.

In fact, it's less so. My Peace Corps years corresponded to a brief period of liberalization in Tibet, following the death of Chinese dictator Mao Zedong. But the Chinese cracked down in the late 1980s and early 1990s, restricting religious practice and Tibetan language instruction. Chinese authorities imposed martial law in the Tibetan capital of Lhasa after riots in 1989 and again in 2008, when hundreds of protesters were killed or detained by security forces.

And last month [March 2012] in New Delhi, to protest the visit of Chinese President Hu Jintao, Tibetan exile Jamphel Yeshi died after setting himself on fire. "We demand freedom to practice our religion and culture," Yeshi wrote, in a letter discovered after his death. "We demand the same right as other people living elsewhere in the world."

Is Anyone Listening?

But the world doesn't seem to be listening. Fearful of upsetting Beijing, Indian authorities imposed their own crackdown on Tibetan exiles during the Hu visit. Nor has the death of

Yeshi—or the 30-odd other Tibetan self-immolations over the past year—drawn much attention in the West, despite opinion polls showing widespread support for Tibetan autonomy and independence.

To be fair, President Barack Obama and other world leaders have periodically called upon China to loosen the reins in Tibet. They also have met with the Tibetans' spiritual leader, the Dalai Lama, who was exiled along with 80,000 followers after a failed uprising in 1959.

A New Strategy

But China continues to turn a deaf ear to the protests. So it's time for a different tack, which is sure to make Beijing sit up and take notice: an international boycott on Chinese-made goods.

It's happened before. In the run-up to the 2008 Beijing Olympics, activists in France and elsewhere pledged not to purchase products made in China. And the Chinese responded in kind, organizing their own boycott against French companies following pro-Tibetan demonstrations at the Olympic torch relay in Paris.

Let's be clear: No matter what happens, the world will keep buying Chinese products.

Most electronic gadgets contain something that is produced in China. So do millions of clothing items, whether their labels say so or not.

A Boycott Is a Powerful Symbol

But a boycott is a good idea anyway, precisely because of its unique symbolic power. Certainly the Chinese recognize that, to judge from their angry response to the Olympic protests.

Second, in this era of social networking, a boycott engages people in the real world instead of just the virtual one. Consider the "KONY 2012" video, documenting the depravities of Ugandan rebel Joseph Kony, which went viral earlier this year and urged viewers to sign Internet petitions. They did. And then the movement fizzled, because it was conducted almost entirely online.

By contrast, a boycott would affect our day-to-day decisions at the most prosaic level: Do I buy a product or not? That's a much more promising formula for long-term change than a few clicks of the mouse.

Raising Awareness

Most of all, a boycott could help inform the world about Tibetans. The Chinese news media continually casts them as ignorant ingrates, so shrouded in Buddhist religious dogma that they can't appreciate the economic benefits that China has brought to them. We need a global campaign to counter that myth, and a boycott has the best chance of sparking it.

Yes, Chinese resources and investment—especially in infrastructure—have helped develop Tibet. But every colonial power uses a similar gambit to justify its rule, as the Chinese should understand better than anyone else. After invading Manchuria in 1931, for example, Japan built a railway and spurred industrialization across the region. But that didn't excuse Japanese torture and other human rights violations against the Chinese, any more than Chinese investments justify repression in Tibet.

Even a pledge to eschew Chinese products might make a difference, whether people actually alter their purchasing habits or not. Consider an April 2001 radio advertisement aired by an American plumbers' union, after China detained 24 airmen from a downed U.S. surveillance plane.

"The crew of an American plane, forced to make an emergency landing in China, is held hostage by the Chinese government," the advertisement declared. "Think about that. And vow to buy no Chinese products until the servicemen and women are released."

A few days later, they were. But millions of Tibetans remain locked in subjugation. Think about that, the next time you go shopping. It won't free Tibet, but it might change a few minds. Including yours.

| "It is possible that China will try to defuse the tensions [in Tibet] by reopening talks with the Dalai Lama's representatives."

China Should Resume Talks with the Dalai Lama

The Economist

The Economist *is a weekly news and international affairs publication based in England. In the following viewpoint, the author observes that the situation in Tibet is dire: Tibetans are increasingly self-immolating to protest harsh Chinese rule and the continuing exile of the Dalai Lama, and Chinese authorities are concerned that the self-immolation protests are spreading and have sharply blamed "the Dalai Clique" for the trend. But it is possible that China will try to defuse the rising tension by reopening talks with the Dalai Lama's representatives, the author contends. Some Tibetans have a renewed glimmer of hope with the appointment of a new Chinese leader, Xi Jinping; however, there is little hope that anything constructive will be accomplished, because there is a lack of international pressure on China to do so.*

As you read, consider the following questions:

1. How many Tibetans have resorted to self-immolation in the past two years, as stated by *The Economist*?

2. When was the last time China held talks with the Dalai Lama's representatives, according to the author?

3. As reported by the author, in what village was the Dalai Lama born?

Inside a small monastery in China's Qinghai province, a red-robed monk looks around to see if he is being watched, then begins sobbing. "We just want the Dalai Lama to come home", he says. His words echo those of dozens of Tibetans seeking to explain why they have set themselves on fire in public places across the Tibetan plateau in the past two years. Desperation is growing among the Dalai Lama's followers in China. So, too, is the government's effort to silence them.

Since an outbreak of unrest swept the Tibetan plateau five years ago this month [March 2013], including anti-Chinese riots in the Tibetan capital Lhasa and protests in numerous towns and monasteries, the party has tried to control Tibetan discontent by means of carrot and stick. The stick has involved tighter policing of monasteries, controls on visits to Lhasa, denunciations of the Dalai Lama and arrests of dissidents. The carrot is visible not far from the crying monk's monastery: new expressways across the vast grasslands, new roads to remote villages, better housing for monks and restorations to their prayer-halls. Yet the spectacle of more than 100 Tibetans setting themselves alight, mostly in the past two years, in one of the largest such protests in modern political history, suggests that neither approach is working.

Despite, or perhaps because of, intense crackdowns in the affected areas of the Tibetan plateau, the burnings in recent months have spread across a wider area (the plateau is one-third the size of America) and involved more people without links to monasteries. The government's growing worry is evident in the intense security in the worst-affected areas, mostly in Tibetan-populated parts of the provinces of Sichuan and Qinghai, as well as in Lhasa, the capital of the Tibet Autonomous Region (TAR). Since last year [2012] the government has begun rounding up those deemed to have encouraged Tibetans to burn themselves. Dozens have been detained. Several have been jailed for terms ranging from a few months to life.

A state of alert

All of the TAR, as well as trouble spots in neighbouring provinces, are off limits to most foreign journalists. But tension is palpable even in the few areas that remain accessible. During celebrations of the Tibetan new year in late February, at least three fire engines were parked inside Kumbum monastery compound near Xining, the capital of Qinghai. Dozens of police with extinguishers and fire blankets stood among the crowds of pilgrims and holidaymakers. West of Xining in Hainan prefecture, a Tibetan-majority area about the size of Switzerland, no one has been reported to have set themselves on fire. But the authorities are worried. In November hundreds of medical students protested in Gonghe county against the circulation of a government leaflet disparaging the immolators and the Dalai Lama. Residents say the police used teargas to break up a demonstration in the county town and arrested several participants. The prefectural authorities called the demonstration "illegal" and demanded that young people in Hainan form a (metaphorical) "wall of copper and rampart of iron against splittism, infiltration and self-immolations".

Though most minority groups live fairly peacefully under Chinese rule, the Tibetans cite many reasons for the renewed unrest: the continuing influx of ethnic-Han migrants (encouraged by huge government investment in transport infrastructure); environmental damage caused by mining and construction; the marginalisation of the Tibetan language in schools. The ageing of the Dalai Lama (he is 77) and his announcement in 2011 that he was retiring as head of Tibet's government-in-exile in India are also factors. A growing sense that this incarnation of the Dalai Lama might not have much longer is fuelling demands for his return to the land that he fled after a failed uprising in 1959.

Too long in exile

"[In] this life . . . service at least in the field of Tibetan struggle now already end", says the Dalai Lama in his halting English in the Indian town of Dharamsala that is his home. He is now, he says, devoting himself to the promotion of religious harmony and a dialogue between Buddhism and modern science. China is not convinced. Robert Barnett of Columbia University says that in recent weeks Chinese officials have increasingly accused the "Dalai Lama clique" of organising the burnings.

Mr Barnett says it is possible that China will try to defuse the tensions by reopening talks with the Dalai Lama's representatives. There have been no such meetings since January 2010, when the two sides reached an impasse over differences relating to the envoys' call for "genuine autonomy" for Tibet, while accepting that it remain part of China. (Other Tibetans in India still want independence, a cause of dispute among the exiles.) Chinese officials denounce even the compromise of autonomy as a scheme for achieving full independence. Among China's other concerns is a proposal that Tibet be defined as the TAR plus the Tibetan-inhabited areas of neighbouring provinces, an area one quarter the size of China.

"Now demon peacefully sleeping"

The Dalai Lama's retirement could make a resumption of talks more difficult. In August 2011, after winning an election in which nearly 50,000 Tibetan exiles voted, Lobsang Sangay, a Harvard academic, took over as head of the exiled govern-

© Cartoonstock.com.

ment and assumed the political role once played by the Dalai Lama ("now demon peacefully sleeping", the holy man quips, referring to a word he says Chinese officials have used to describe him). Mr Sangay says that China can still hold talks if it wants with the Dalai Lama's representatives. But those envoys resigned in June, citing the "deteriorating situation" in Tibet and China's failure to "respond positively" to autonomy proposals. Among the powers Mr Sangay has taken on is the right to appoint the envoys' successors, who have yet to be chosen. This will make China wary of beginning talks, for fear of conferring legitimacy on the new exile administration.

Some Tibetans in India see a glimmer of hope in China's ten-yearly change of leadership which will be completed with the appointments of Xi Jinping as president and Li Keqiang as prime minister shortly before the end of the annual session of China's parliament, the National People's Congress, on March 17th. Mr Xi's predecessor, Hu Jintao, was party chief in Tibet during an outbreak of unrest in the late 1980s which he resolutely suppressed (just as he suppressed the far bigger eruption in 2008). Mr Xi, goes the thinking, could be different. In the 1950s the Dalai Lama got to know Mr Xi's late father, Xi Zhongxun, who was one of Mao Zedong's comrades. The elder Xi received a watch from the Dalai Lama, which he wore long after the flight to India. If the father had a soft spot for the Dalai Lama, optimists think, so might the son.

Interesting developments

In recent months the birthplace of the Dalai Lama in Hongya village, about 30km (20 miles) south-east of Kumbum monastery, has been given a makeover, though no one is sure why. Despite a crackdown on Dalai Lama worship elsewhere on the plateau, visitors to the grey-walled compound can see photographs of him, as well as a golden throne intended for him to sit on should he ever return. A caretaker says money for the recent improvements (including new bricks and a coat of paint) came from the government. She says foreigners are not allowed inside, but gladly shows around a group of Tibetan pilgrims who have driven hundreds of kilometres to see the site. But exiled officials are unimpressed and the Dalai Lama is cautious. "Better to wait till some concrete things happen, otherwise . . . some disappointment", he says with a chuckle.

Indeed, disappointment still appears likely. Mr Xi is under little pressure from other countries to change Chinese policy on Tibet. The unrest in 2008 broke out as China was preparing to host the Olympic games. It wanted the event to mark the country's emergence as an open-minded world power. Despite that, it cracked down hard on the protests, but in a concession to international demands, resumed talks with the Dalai Lama's representatives less than two months later. Two rounds were held before the games started, but with no obvious progress.

Since 2008 the West's economic malaise has made China even less amenable to foreign persuasion on Tibet. Britain, hoping to reduce China's prickliness on the issue, announced in October that year that it was abandoning its century-old policy (unique among Western countries) of merely recognising China's "suzerainty" over the region rather than its sovereignty. It has reaped no obvious reward. Britain's relations with China were plunged into a prolonged chill by a meeting last May [2012] between the Dalai Lama and the British prime minister, David Cameron. *Global Times*, a Beijing newspaper, said last month that China had "more leverage than Britain" in the two countries' relations, adding with some justification: "Few countries can afford to really be tough against China."

One nation indivisible

Mr Xi faces little pressure from public or elite opinion inside China, other than to maintain a firm grip. Some Chinese intellectuals have questioned whether the government's heavy-handedness in Tibet will bring about long-lasting stability. A small but seemingly growing number of Han Chinese, the country's ethnic majority, are attracted by Tibetan Buddhism (Han visitors to Kumbum Monastery thronged around its statues and clasped their hands in prayer during the recent festivities). But concessions to the Dalai Lama on autonomy have little support in China.

Few observers expect any relaxation of what seems to be a stepped-up effort to stop Tibetans fleeing to India. Before 2008, 2,000–3,000 a year were doing so. This fell to a few hundred after the unrest that year. A new refugee centre opened in Dharamsala in 2011, with American funding and the capacity for 500 people. In 2012 fewer than 400 escaped. At the beginning of March only two people—a couple from a Tibetan area of Sichuan province—were there. Before they left their village, they had to sign a document saying they would not go to India. For Tibetans, even visiting Lhasa needs a permit. Last year hundreds were detained, some of them for months, after returning from legal trips to India in which they surreptitiously attended teachings by the Dalai Lama in Bodh Gaya, a holy Buddhist site.

Heavy security in Tibet, including riot police patrolling the streets of Lhasa, may help prevent another plateau-wide explosion like that of 2008. But the sight of Tibetans setting themselves on fire, and official attempts to denigrate them, are deepening the region's wounds. Little chance of resolution is in sight. The weeping monk recalls that, after an earthquake in 2010 in Qinghai's Yushu county, officials asked some victims what they needed. They replied that they just wanted the Dalai Lama back. "They can control us," the monk says, "but they can't control our hearts."

> "What a routinisation of self-immolation as political protest can lead to the Chinese authorities may not be even able to comprehend."

The Political Psychology of Self-Immolation

Costica Bradatan

Costica Bradatan is an author and fellow at the Notre Dame Institute for Advanced Study in South Bend, Indiana. In the following viewpoint, he finds self-immolation to be an extraordinary political protest because it strikes a chord within the human psyche and provides a glimpse "into the primordial experience of the sacred." It has also been the catalyst for serious political change in some instances; in others, self-immolation has failed to spark revolution or major political or social reforms. In Tibet, the growing wave of self-immolations has yet to result in significant political change. Yet the Chinese authorities should not grow complacent and consider such extraordinary protests as routine, because the act of self-immolation signals a desperation that can erupt into a full-fledged crisis.

As you read, consider the following questions:

1. What self-immolation death did the American journalist David Halberstam describe, according to the author?

2. How many self-immolations may have taken place from 1963 to 2003, in Bradatan's opinion?

3. How many Tibetans have resorted to self-immolation from 2009 to 2012, as reported by the author?

Here he is. Matches in one hand, petrol bottle in the other. He removes the bottle cap, drops it to the ground and douses himself in liquid. He does everything slowly, methodically, as if it were part of a routine he has practiced for years. Then he stops, looks around, and strikes a match.

At this moment nothing in the world can bridge the gap that separates the self-immolator from the others. His total defiance of the survival and self-preservation instincts, his determination to trample on what everybody else finds precious, the ease with which he seems to dispose of his own life, all these place him not only beyond our capacity of understanding, but also outside of human society. He now inhabits a place that most of us find uninhabitable. Yet, from there he does not cease to dominate us.

Journalist David Halberstam describes the death of Thích Quàng Dúc, the Vietnamese Buddhist monk who set himself on fire in Saigon in 1963. The quieter the self-immolator the more agitated those around him. The former may slip into nothingness, but his performance changes the latter's lives forever. They experience repulsion and attraction, terror and boundless reverence, awe and fear, all at once. Over them he now has the uncanniest form of power.

> "As he burned he never moved a muscle, never uttered a sound, his outward composure in sharp contrast to the wailing people around him."

The experience is so powerful because it is so deeply seated in the human psyche. In front of self-immolation, even the most secularized of us have a glimpse into a primordial experience of the sacred. Originally, the sacred is defined as something set apart, cut off from the rest, which remains profane; what we feel towards such a radically different other is precisely a mix of terror and fascination. Self-immolation is a unique event precisely because it awakens deep layers of our ultimate make-up. In a striking, if disguised fashion, self-immolation occasions the experience of the sacred even in a God-forsaken world like ours.

Self-immolation has little to do with suicide. "Suicidal tendencies almost never lead to self-immolation," says Michael Biggs, one of the few sociologists who have studied the phenomenon systematically. Self-immolation is a deliberate, determined and painfully expressive form of individual protest. Under certain circumstances, the gesture of an individual self-immolator is enough to ignite large-scale social movements. Thích Quảng Dúc's self-immolation triggered a massive response, which resulted in the toppling of the Ngô Dình Diem regime in South Vietnam. Only six years later, Jan Palach, a Czech philosophy student, set himself ablaze in protest to the Soviet Union's crush of the Prague Spring. His death did not cause a regime change right away, but it shaped in a distinct manner the anti-communist dissidence in Czechoslovakia. Twenty years later, in 1989, it was a "Palach week" of street protests and demonstrations that set in motion the Velvet Revolution. More recently, in December 2010, Mohamed Bouazizi, a young Tunisian street vendor, struck a match that not only burned him to death, but set the entire Arab world on fire; we are still witnessing the aftermath of his gesture.

Self-immolation is a fearsome, compelling act, but it would be wrong to infer that whenever it occurs it has significant political consequences. Michael Biggs estimates that between 800 and 3,000 self-immolations may have taken place over the

Map of Tibetan Self-Immolations

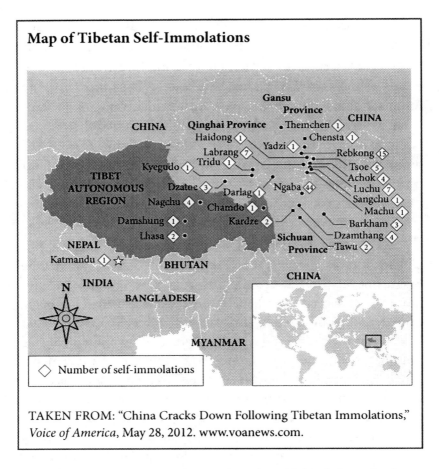

TAKEN FROM: "China Cracks Down Following Tibetan Immolations," *Voice of America*, May 28, 2012. www.voanews.com.

four decades after 1963. Yet, only a handful of them had any political impact. What makes a death by self-immolation politically consequential is its capacity to become the focus of a community's social life. Self-immolation is "successful" in this sense when it is not anymore about the one who performs it, but about the community in the midst of which it occurs and which suddenly recognizes itself in the predicament of the self-immolator, it feels "shamed" by his gesture and compelled to act. Thus, that individual death is re-signified, and turned from a biological occurrence in the history of someone's body into a "founding" event of mythical proportions, something that renews the community's political life.

Politically "successful" self-immolations are extraordinary events. There are no "recipes for success" here; no science can satisfactorily explain when they should occur or why they shouldn't. To use some kind of analogy, they are not unlike artistic masterpieces; you can recognize one when you see it, but they cannot be produced "on demand". As such, they are inimitable and unrepeatable. Bouazizi, Dúc and Palach had many imitators, but they never managed to get out of their masters' shadows; the more they were the less their gestures meant.

This brings home the point that a politically consequential self-immolation is usually the first one in a series. Since February 2009 no less than fifty-one Tibetans, mostly Buddhist monks and nuns, have self-immolated in Tibetan parts of China, yet they have not caused any significant political changes so far. Why? Because fifty-one self-immolations may be fifty too many; the more Tibetans self-immolate the clearer it becomes that there are no Quàng Dúc, Jan Palach or Mohamed Bouazizi among them.

The fact that self-immolation as a form of political protest could even appear in Tibetan monastic circles may seem puzzling. Buddhism notoriously rejects violence; moreover, Tibetan Buddhism is eminently based on compassion towards all sentient beings. One of the four vows that any Tibetan monk has to take when joining a monastery is "never to take a life". The Dalai Lama's total embrace of Gandhi's *satyagraha* is only the logical corollary of such a religious mind-set.

Yet, the explanation has to do more with political, rather than theological, factors. The Chinese occupation of Tibet has been unusually oppressive and much of the violent repression has been directed against Buddhist monasteries, seen as the symbol of a "backward," "feudal" Tibet. Violence only breeds violence. For all its anti-violent stance, when its very existence comes under threat, Buddhism could sometimes find the resources, and even the theoretical justification, for violent resistance; the PLA experienced this first-hand in the Tibet of the 1950s, when monasteries would often fight back. Moreover, most of the recent self-immolations have taken place in what used to be, before the communist take-over, Amdo and Kham, regions populated by fiercely independent people, combination of warriors and monks, that almost no central authority could subdue in the past. The Kampas could be as brutal as the PLA soldiers.

That self-immolation, by all means an extreme and extraordinary act, tends now to become a routine form of political action is a very dangerous development. And, yet, just as the Chinese authorities do not signal that they want to make concessions, the Tibetans find it inconceivable to give up. The fact that all those who set themselves ablaze are young (some are teens) is telling. These are people who don't have the memory of a pre-communist Tibet; all they could possibly have is the hope of a post-Chinese one. But, then again, with Tibet's new demographic structure and China's super-power status, even such a hope is unsustainable. So all they are left with is despair.

In the long-run Tibetans' despair may be China's worst nightmare. What a routinisation of self-immolation as political protest can lead to the Chinese authorities may not be even able to comprehend. And, yet, they should not be surprised; maybe it is time they start re-reading the little red book: "Where there is oppression, there is resistance." In his grave, Mao Zedong is dreaming in Tibetan.

| "Many exiled Tibetan intellectuals consider social media to have transformed the Free Tibet movement."

Social Media Have Mobilized Support for the Free Tibet Movement

Saransh Seghal

Saransh Seghal is a journalist and student. In the following viewpoint, he reports that growing numbers of Tibetan exiles and Tibetans in Tibet are turning to social media to promote activism and political change. For Tibetan exiles, social media are an effective way to advocate Tibetan independence and garner support. For Tibetans in Tibet, it is the best way to communicate with the outside world, even if they have to find ways to avoid China's online surveillance and censorship. According to some activists, the disadvantage of the rising popularity of using social media for political purposes is it diminishes participation in street rallies and protests, muting the power of such activities.

As you read, consider the following questions:

1. What is the capital of the exiled Tibetan community in India, as stated by Seghal?

2. How many Tibetans are there in Tibet, according to the author?

3. When did Tibetans inside Tibet begin to utilize social media to disseminate information and stay in touch with Tibetans in exile, according to Seghal?

Frustrated by the fact that their Free Tibet movement is increasingly losing its international attractiveness in the real world, many young exiled Tibetan activists are turning to the virtual world by making use of social media to seek support and advocate their cause for Rangzen (a fully independent Tibet).

A Declining Movement

But critics doubt the effectiveness of their new strategy, saying indulgence in the virtual world without real action could eventually turn the Free Tibet movement into a virtual one of self-consolation. It is a fact in the real world today that many governments want to maintain good relations with China, the world's second-largest economy. As such, they no longer highlight the human-rights issue when dealing with Beijing. As a result, the Tibet issue becomes less and less significant in major powers' policies toward China. Particularly after the political retirement this year [2011] of the Dalai Lama, the exiled Tibetan spiritual leader, the Tibet issue seems to be increasingly fading from the international arena.

Nowadays, campaigns for solidarity, candlelight vigils and protests organized by exiled Tibetans and their supporters outside Chinese embassies and at international events or even self-immolations by Tibetans inside China hardly make headlines in international mainstream media.

A Virtual World

Fearing that the Free Tibet movement will soon be forgotten, many frustrated exiled Tibetan activists and their supporters now resort to the virtual world in hopes that they can keep the momentum of their cause by spreading information through social media. Even inside China, despite Beijing's tough controls on the Internet, some Tibetans risk their freedom and even their lives to send out information via virtual private networks and Internet proxies, such as photos and videos of self-immolations and protests against the central government's repressive policies.

But it is in Dharamsala, the capital of the exiled Tibetan community in the Indian Himalayas, from where a byte of information uploaded on the Internet can spread globally within seconds to reach Free Tibet sympathizers and supporters. Many young Tibetans in exile and their supporters can then quickly relay the information through social media, hoping that it can spread worldwide and even penetrate China itself to arouse the attention of concerned people.

The exiles believe that in this way they can make the sufferings of Tibetans inside China known worldwide, to awaken the consciences of those who still care about human rights in Tibet.

Although they have little direct contact with the 6 million Tibetans still in their homeland, the exiles maintain good connections and communication with their supporters around the world through social networks such as Facebook, Twitter and YouTube. Tragic videos of monks and nuns setting themselves on fire have a shocking impression on viewers. Many exiled Tibetans believe that such a modern approach can more effectively let the world see the grim reality inside Tibet and arouse sympathy.

"As a Tibetan working for the [Free Tibet] cause, I see social media not just as an intermediary to relay news stories but also as an important and effective tool to directly connect individuals together and mobilize the overseas Tibetan diaspora community, and to awaken global awareness on the Tibet issue. Social media also give an opportunity for exiled Tibetans to build a link with Tibetans inside Tibet despite

China's great firewall," says Dharamsala-based Tsering Choe-dup, the Asia regional coordinator at International Tibet Network, a non-governmental organization aimed at maximizing the effectiveness of the worldwide Tibet movement.

The Role of Social Media

The development of social media within the exiled Tibetan community started during the Beijing Olympics in 2008 and grew rapidly during the exile community's general elections in 2011.

Beijing also understands the power of the new technology and has recently announced plans to strengthen control on the Internet further and scan micro-blogging sites frequently used by Tibetans. However, news stories about troubles in Tibet still manage to be sent out. The Chinese government constantly blames the Dalai Lama and overseas Tibetans for making trouble inside the region.

A good example of Beijing's cyber-control is how it deals with Tsering Woeser, a Tibetan poet, writer and blogger currently living in Beijing who supports human rights inside Tibet. Woeser keeps updating news on her weblog *Invisible Tibet*. As a result, Chinese authorities keep a close watch on her and often put her under house arrest.

Leading activist groups such as the Tibetan Youth Congress, Students for a Free Tibet, the Tibetan Women's Association and various others have fomed social media groups and conduct online campaigning. Interestingly, many young radical Tibetans have Rangzen as their middle names on Facebook and other social websites.

New Strategies

Shibayan Raha, an Indian online organizer and firm supporter of the Free Tibet movement, says: "Social media are changing the [methods] and the face of the movement. Since 2008, Ti-

China and Internet Censorship

Some of the world's governments seek to censor, intercept, decode, disrupt, guard, or otherwise control Internet traffic. In several countries, Internet control implies the monitoring and control of the Internet behaviors of its citizens. For example, the government of China employs more than 30,000 full-time workers to monitor Internet systems accessed by the country's 250 million Web users. In the past, China has periodically blocked access to various websites, including Wikipedia, United Nations News, and the human-rights group Amnesty International. The OpenNet Initiative asserts that close to forty-five countries filter or heavily censor the Internet for political content or individual speech. Most countries have restrictive Internet laws that limit the content available to children in school or ban the illegal transfer of copyrighted materials.

Global Issues in Context,
"Internet Control and Security," 2013.
www.gale.cengage.com.

betans inside Tibet have used social media on a daily basis to communicate with the outside world, especially exiled activists from the movement.

"At the same time we can see how Tibetans inside Tibet are remarkably using these very same services on a proxy server and sending out information. Most of the self-immolation pictures, news [and] videos have come through social media websites.

"China surely has tried hard to curb these activities, but it apparently [has failed] miserably. The news is being carried all over the world."

The Tibetan diaspora is paradoxically claimed as the most successful refugee community in the world, and the Internet has become increasingly important in the lives of many refugees, often termed "the digital diaspora." Online anti-China campaigns run on social-media platforms have proliferated within Tibetan exile communities across the world and among their overseas friends. Tibetan monks and nuns, despite their strict monastic lifestyle, too have started embracing social-media technology, and thousands of them are seen sharing information and commenting on Facebook. Many informative websites have also come up with Chinese-language versions to reach out to the Chinese public.

Staying Connected

Many exiled Tibetan intellectuals consider social media to have transformed the Free Tibet movement, so expect it to continue.

Phurbu Thinley, a well-known Tibetan journalist based in Dharamsala, believes that "for Tibetans, it is the way forward to resort to all kinds of peaceful approaches. . . . Social media have become a convenient alternative source and vehicle of information for the scattered exiled Tibetan community and their supporters around the world. They also make such information open to more open-minded Chinese people in China and abroad.

"Social media, when used effectively, [constitute] a powerful tool to promote activism and change, and even to ignite large unprecedented public events. Tibetans are aware of this. Tibetans are aware of the role played by social networks during the uprisings in the Arab world," Thinley adds.

The Limitations of Social Media

But not all campaigners believe this is going in the right direction. Joe Hamilton, a German supporter of the Free Tibet movement, says: "Of course people do get the chance to access videos and information. However, this is all about communication. It is not as strong as participating in protests; with a click people [think] they have contributed. The outcome won't be as strong as listening to a Tibetan monk or nun telling their story. The only tool is the street; hit the streets and change will come."

Dibyesh Anand, associate professor in international relations at the University of Westminster, who recently hosted the Dalai Lama's talk on "Values of Democracy and Tibet" at the London institution, says: "Social media no doubt facilitate dissemination of information and mobilization of activists by reducing the time and cost of doing so. However, they do not make revolutions, nor do they bring meaningful change. It is people on the street alone who can force a significant change in states' policies.

"If we take the example of the use of social media by Tibetans and their supporters, my impression is that the circle within which the images and stories circulate remains confined. That is, very few non-supporters are converted to the cause. Social media allow us to live in a bubble of active cybercitizenry.

"But this should not give a false illusion that there are more supporters for the Tibetan cause due to social media than there were without it. Social media are especifically insignificant when it comes to the Tibetan issue because they face severe restrictions in Chinese-controlled Tibet, where most Tibetans live. That Tibetans in diaspora use them extensively and thus create a cyber-nation is an interesting phenomenon, but nowhere as important as protests and resistance inside Tibet. So a cautionary tale of social media and Tibet is better than a celebratory one."

However, while the exiled Tibetans remain in an imbroglio over how to carry on their movement and find a possible solution to win freedom for their homeland so that they can go back together with the Dalai Lama, many believe tech-savvy work will help their struggle and raise publicity for their cause.

Periodical and Internet Sources Bibliography

The following articles have been selected to supplement the diverse views presented in this chapter.

Jeffrey Bartholet	"Aflame," *New Yorker*, July 8, 2013.
Nilanjana Bhowmick	"Tibetans Turn to Alternative Protest as Self-Immolations Prove Futile," *Time*, April 17, 2013.
Patrick Brown	"Tibet's Epidemic of Self-Immolation," CBC News, February 14, 2013. www.cbc.ca.
Allen Carlson	"Moving Past the Wreckage of China's Tibet Policy," *The Diplomat*, March 29, 2013. http://thediplomat.com.
China.org.cn	"Self-Immolation Truth: Tibetan Buddhism Kidnapped by Politics," July 19, 2012. www.china.org.cn.
Hua Zi	"Extreme Acts of Violence," China.org.cn, November 25, 2011.
Yanzhong Huang	"The Dalai Lama's Self-Immolation Dilemma," Council on Foreign Relations, May 13, 2013. www.cfr.org.
Tenzing Lhamo	"For Them, We Have to Act," Tibet Sun, February 14, 2013. www.tibetsun.com.
Sue Lloyd-Roberts	"Self-Immolations Shake Tibetan Resolve," BBC News, April 18, 2012. www.bbc.co.uk.
Carole McGranahan and Ralph Litzinger	"Self-Immolation as Protest in Tibet," *Cultural Anthropology*, April 9, 2012.
Thuy Ong	"Tibetan Self-Immolations Having Little Effect, Dalai Lama Says," Reuters, June 13, 2013. www.reuters.com.

For Further Discussion

Chapter 1

1. The first three viewpoints in this chapter examine the question of Tibet's sovereignty. Which option do you believe is the best one for Tibet? Why?

2. Isabel Hilton contends that the Dalai Lama has been an effective leader of the Tibetan people. In his viewpoint, Andy Lamey criticizes the Dalai Lama's leadership. Which writer makes the more persuasive argument? Explain.

Chapter 2

1. The impact of Chinese rule on Tibet's fragile environment has been a global issue of concern. After reading the viewpoints by George Schaller and Y.C. Dhardhowa, do you believe that China is devastating Tibet's environment? Or is China aiding in major conservation efforts? Explain.

2. What is the reason for the shocking trend of self-immolations in Tibet? Lois Farrow Parshley attributes the rise in self-immolation protests to China's oppressive rule. Pankaj Mishra argues that globalization and modernization plays a major role in the trend. Consider each view to make an informed opinion on the matter.

Chapter 3

1. Which viewpoint in this chapter do you believe would be the most effective way that the United States could engage Tibet? Which would be the least effective? Explain your answers.

2. Should the Tibetan Policy Act be strengthened, as Richard Gere argues in his viewpoint? Or do you agree with Daniel Baer that the US is adequately and aggressively

responding to the Tibet crisis under the current act? What aspects of the legislation could be strengthened, if any, in your opinion? Why?

Chapter 4

1. In recent months, global attention has turned to the rising rate of self-immolations in Tibet. Costica Bradatan asserts that such protests can be effective in raising awareness and spurring political change. What is your opinion on self-immolation as political protest?

2. The viewpoints in this chapter examine several ways in which to encourage political change in Tibet. Identify the two that you believe could be most effective and explain why. Use information from the viewpoints in your answer.

Organizations to Contact

The editors have compiled the following list of organizations concerned with the issues debated in this book. The descriptions are derived from materials provided by the organizations. All have publications or information available for interested readers. The list was compiled on the date of publication of the present volume; names, addresses, phone and fax numbers, and e-mail and Internet addresses may change. Be aware that many organizations take several weeks or longer to respond to inquiries, so allow as much time as possible.

Central Tibetan Administration (CTA)
Office of Information & International Relations
Dharamsala, HP   176215
　India
91 1892 222457 • fax: 91 1892 224957
e-mail: diir@tibet.net
website: http://tibet.net

Regarded as Tibet's government in exile, the Central Tibetan Administration (CTA) was created by the Dalai Lama in 1959 in Dharamsala, at the foot of the Himalayas. The CTA advocates for Tibetan democratic self-governance, rehabilitates and educates Tibetan refugees, offers health services, promotes Tibetan culture and language, and disseminates the work of the Dalai Lama and elected CTA officials. There are thousands of Tibetan refugees living in countries all over the world (the Tibetan diaspora), and the CTA works to give those refugees a voice in Tibet's future and to provide them with crucial resources. It also works with international organizations, nongovernmental organizations (NGOs), national governments, and global activists to bring about Tibet's political autonomy from China and the end to political and cultural oppression in Tibet. The CTA website provides access to statements from the Dalai Lama and other CTA officials; a TibetOnline TV archive; reports, commentaries, and environmental studies; and links to periodicals, including *Green Tibet* and the *Tibetan Bulletin*.

Conservancy for Tibetan Art and Culture (CTAC)

1825 Eye Street NW, Suite 400, Washington, DC 20006
(202) 828-6288 • fax: (703) 538-4671
e-mail: info@tibetanculture.org
website: www.tibetanculture.org

The Conservancy for Tibetan Art and Culture (CTAC) is a nonprofit organization established in 1997 to preserve and promote Tibetan art and culture. It works with Tibetan artists, officials, international scholars, and leading institutions to organize seminars, exhibitions, and symposia; provides educational resources for educators and those in cultural fields; and sponsors cultural research into Tibet's rich heritage. According to the organization's website, "To preserve a millennium of cultural heritage the Conservancy works in remote and sensitive areas on the Tibetan plateau to identify, document, and help protect historically and culturally significant pilgrimage sites, shrines, monasteries, nunneries, artwork and rare texts." The CTAC website provides information on the group's programs, ongoing initiatives, and upcoming events.

Free Tibet Campaign

28 Charles Square, London N1 5HT
  United Kingdom
44 020 7324 4605
e-mail: alistair@freetibet.org
website: www.freetibet.org

The Free Tibet Campaign is a nonprofit, nongovernmental organization that works for Tibetan independence and the end to human rights abuses by the Chinese against the Tibetan people. Key to its mission is the education of the public on the need for Tibetan political and cultural self-determination; an end to torture and widespread imprisonment of Tibetan political activists; and the importance of freedom of religion. Free Tibet actively lobbies the British Parliament to support its efforts to help the Tibetan people, especially when it comes to ending Chinese human rights abuses, with the long-term goal of ending Chinese occupation of the country. The Free Tibet website outlines recent campaigns, including efforts to release political prisoners from jail and organizing boycotts of companies that exploit the suffering of the Tibetan people.

International Campaign for Tibet (ICT)
1825 Jefferson Place NW, Washington, DC   20036
(202) 785-1515 • fax: (202) 785-4343
e-mail: info@savetibet.org
website: www.savetibet.org

The International Campaign (ICT) for Tibet was founded in 1988 to "promote human rights and democratic freedoms for the people of Tibet." It investigates and monitors human rights, socioeconomic, and environmental conditions in the country; lobbies Western countries to develop and support policies to help the Tibetan people and encourage political self-determination; works to release Tibetan political prisoners; advocates for religious freedom and democratic reform in Tibet; and mobilizes support for Tibetan refugees and citizens fleeing from religious and/or political oppression. The ICT also practices Chinese outreach by translating information on China's rule of Tibet and disseminating it to the Chinese media, organizations, activists, government officials, and other interested parties. Education and outreach are two of the ICT's main goals. To that end, it offers fact sheets, reports, videos, congressional testimony, speeches, papers, and other material. The ICT also offers access to the organization's e-newsletters: *Tibetan Press Watch* and *Tibetan Brief*.

Students for a Free Tibet (SFT)
602 East Fourteenth Street, 2nd Floor, New York, NY   10009
(212) 358-0071 • fax: (212) 358-1771
e-mail: info@studentsforafreetibet.org
website: www.studentsforafreetibet.org

Students for a Free Tibet (SFT) is a network of young student activists and Tibetan refugees throughout the world focused on helping the Tibetan people attain their freedom and independence from Chinese rule. Recent SFT efforts include training Tibetan monks, nuns, and activists to communicate more securely and efficiently with cutting-edge mobile technology; launching an online news program to analyze and discuss the current state of Tibetan politics and culture; organizing protests of Chinese officials; and lobbying the US Congress and the United Nations. The SFT is also actively supporting Tibet's cultural renaissance by promoting poetry, writing, and music banned under Chinese occupation. The SFT website features the organizations e-newsletter, information on recent campaigns, press releases and reports, and analysis and commentary.

The Tibet Fund
241 East Thirty-Second Street, New York, NY   10016
(212) 213-5011 • fax: (212) 213-1219
e-mail: info@tibetfund.org
website: www.tibetfund.org

The Tibet Fund is a charitable organization dedicated to preserving Tibet's unique cultural and national identity. Funded by international organizations and national governments, The Tibet Fund offers grants to fund health-care and educational programs in Tibet, and it created the Tibetan Scholarship Fund, which brings Tibetan refugees to the United States to pursue graduate studies. It also supports community and economic development efforts that do not threaten the long-term sustainability of Tibet's environment, culture, or national identity. The Tibet Fund works very closely with the Central Tibetan Administration to identify ways to best address Tibet's most pressing needs and then formulates campaigns and policies to make a real difference on the ground.

Tibet House
22 West Fifteenth Street, New York, NY   10011
(212) 807-0563 • fax: (212) 807-0565
website: http://tibethouse.us

Tibet House is an online resource for those interested in Tibetan art and culture. It is dedicated to preserving Tibet's rich cultural heritage by providing an archive and cultural center for art, photographs, music, writing, poetry, and other forms of artistic expression oppressed under Chinese occupation. Tibet House's archive aids researchers and educators and inspires students and art lovers from around the world. The ultimate aim is to create an extensive online museum and educational programs on Tibetan history, art, and culture. Tibet House holds an annual concert in New York City and hosts a wide range of events to support its programs.

Tibet Justice Center (TJC)
440 Grand Avenue, Suite 425, Oakland, CA   94610
(510) 486-0588
e-mail: tjc@tibetjustice.org
website: www.tibetjustice.org

The Tibet Justice Center (TJC) is a nonprofit legal organization that works to protect the human rights of Tibetan people and to advocate for Tibetan political self-determination. It works with the Central Tibetan Administration (CTA) to help Tibetan refugees and safeguard human rights of Tibetans under Chinese rule; investigates and disseminates the status of human rights, environmental protections, and religious freedoms to the United Nations, the media, and activists; promotes sustainable development practices on the Tibetan Plateau; and assists the CTA in building and strengthening democratic institutions in the Tibetan diaspora. The TJC website features a range of reports and publications, including United Nations briefing papers, fact sheets, investigative reports, and in-depth studies of issues impacting Tibetan women and children.

Tibetan Youth Congress (TYC)
Central Executive Committee, McLeod Ganj
Dharamsala, HP   176 219
   India

91 1892 221554
e-mail: tyc@tibetanyouthcongress.org
website: tibetanyouthcongress.org

Established in 1970, the Tibetan Youth Congress (TYC) is an international nongovernmental organization of Tibetan exiles dedicated to attaining Tibet's independence from Chinese rule. To that end, the TYC organizes a number of educational activities, including Tibetan art and cultural festivals and health programs for Tibetan exiles, to raise awareness of Tibet's struggles under Chinese oppression and the challenges of the Tibetan diaspora. The TYC publishes an influential quarterly journal, *Rangzen*, which is available on the group's website. Current news, opinion and commentary, press releases, fact sheets, brochures, photos, audio, and video can also be accessed on the website.

US Department of State

2201 C Street NW, Washington, DC   20520
(202) 647-4000
website: www.state.gov

The US Department of State is the federal agency that is responsible for formulating, implementing, and assessing US foreign policy. The State Department also assists US citizens living or traveling abroad, promotes and protects US business interests all over the world, and supports the activities of other US government agencies in foreign countries. The State Department has launched ongoing diplomatic efforts with China regarding the Tibet crisis and informs the US Congress, the president, and the public about the political, economic, and social events in the region. The State Department website features a wealth of information on current policies, upcoming events, daily schedules of top officials, and updates from various countries. It also offers video, congressional testimony, speech transcripts, background notes, human rights reports, and strategy reviews.

Bibliography of Books

Stan Biderman — *Bullet Trains to Yaks: Glimpses into Art, Politics, and Culture in China and Tibet*. Santa Fe, NM: Irony Press, 2011.

Phil Borges — *Tibet: Culture on the Edge*. New York: Rizzoli, 2011.

Yangzom Brauen — *Across Many Mountains: A Tibetan Family's Epic Journey from Oppression to Freedom*. New York: St. Martin's, 2011.

Robert Byron — *First Russia, Then Tibet: Travels Through a Changing World*. London: Tauris Parke, 2011.

Lawrence Davidson — *Cultural Genocide*. New Brunswick, NJ: Rutgers University Press, 2012.

Randall Doyle and Zhang Boshu — *Modern China and the New World: The Reemergence of the Middle Kingdom in the Twenty-First Century*. Lanham, MD: Lexington Books, 2011.

Andrew Martin Fischer — *The Disempowered Development of Tibet in China: A Study in the Economics of Marginalization*. Lanham, MD: Lexington Books, 2013.

Clare E. Harris — *The Museum on the Roof of the World: Art, Politics, and the Representation of Tibet*. Chicago: University of Chicago Press, 2012.

Tim Johnson — *Tragedy in Crimson: How the Dalai Lama Conquered the World but Lost the Battle with China.* New York: Nation Books, 2011.

Anupma Kaushik — *Tibet: In Search of a Solution.* Delhi: Kalinga, 2012.

John Kenneth Knaus — *Beyond Shangri-La: America and Tibet's Move into the Twenty-First Century.* Durham, NC: Duke University Press, 2012.

Michael Lempert — *Discipline and Debate: The Language of Violence in a Tibetan Buddhist Monastery.* Berkley: University of California Press, 2012.

Parshotam Mehra — *Tibet: Writings on History and Politics.* New Delhi: Oxford University Press, 2012.

Andrew J. Nathan and Andrew Scobell — *China's Search for Security.* New York: Columbia University Press, 2012.

Tom Neuhaus — *Tibet in the Western Imagination.* New York: Palgrave Macmillan, 2012.

Jason Q. Ng — *Blocked on Weibo: What Gets Suppressed on China's Version of Twitter (and Why).* New York: New Press, 2013.

Matteo Pistono — *In the Shadow of Buddha: Secret Journeys, Sacred Histories, and Spiritual Discovery in Tibet.* New York: Dutton, 2011.

George B. Schaller — *Tibet Wild: A Naturalist's Journeys on the Roof of the World*. Washington, DC: Island, 2012.

Warren W. Smith Jr. — *China's Tibet? Autonomy or Assimilation*. Lanham, MD: Rowman & Littlefield, 2009.

Sam Van Schaik — *Tibet: A History*. New Haven, CT: Yale University Press, 2011.

Ezra F. Vogel — *Deng Xiaoping and the Transformation of China*. Cambridge, MA: Belknap Press of Harvard University Press, 2011.

Jodi L. Weinstein — *Empire and Identity in Guizhou: Local Resistance to Qing Expansion*. Seattle: University of Washington Press, 2014.

Emily T. Yeh — *Taming Tibet: Landscape Transformation and the Gift of Chinese Development*. Ithaca, NY: Cornell University Press, 2013.

Index

See also Ngawang Lobsang Gyatso, Fifth Dalai Lama; Thubten Gyatso, Thirteenth Dalai Lama
Dhardhowa, Y.C., 93–98
Draft Constitution for a Future Tibet (1963), 75, 79
Drogon Choegyal Phagpa, 73

E

East Asian Legal Studies Program (Harvard Law School), 68, 128–129
The Economist, 181–188
Eleventh Assembly of Tibetan People's Deputies (ATPD), 75
Environment of Tibet
China's destruction of, 93–98
China's preservation efforts, 84–92
destruction through rights violations, 37–38, 37–38
efforts at keeping harmony, 60
highway project destruction, 96–97
mining consequences, 95–96
monitoring efforts, 91
role of religion, 91
water scheme of China, 97
Ethnic cleansing, 95

F

Facebook, 197, 198, 200
First Tibetan General Meeting (2010), 77
The Force of Obedience (Hibou), 110
Foreign Relations Authorization Act (US), 121, 135–136
Free Tibet movement, 57, 150, 177
collective punishments against, 148
death of protestors, 147, 148–149
declining membership, 196
leadership by Dalai Lama, 57
student membership, 198
support for, by social media, 195–202
transition to virtual world, 196–197

G

Ganden Phodrang Government, 74, 79
Gandhi, Mohandas, 60, 193
Gedhun Choekyi Nyima. *See* Panchen Lama of Tibetan Buddhism
Gelugpa lineage of Tibetan Buddhism, 24, 50, 51
Genghis Khan, 19, 73
Genocide. *See* Cultural genocide against Tibet; Natural resource genocide, against Tibet
Gere, Richard, 61, 123–138
Globalization, influence on self-immolation, 106–111
Great Britain
agreement with China, 187
call for Tibet aid, 174
formal recognition of Tibet, 170
military conflicts with Tibet, 62
treaty with Tibet, 34
Guidelines for Future Tibet's Polity (1992), 79

V

W

X

Y

Z